WELCOME TO:
MINGLE TO MILLIONS!

The Art and Science of Building Business
Relationships and Mastering Referrals.

Cami Baker

CamiBaker.com
Cami@CamiBaker.com
(603) 785 - 2598

What Others Are Saying About Cami Baker and This Book:

"As a speaker, author, and business woman, I have spent all my adult life in the line of fire of *networking*. In fact, I, myself, have taught networking tricks and tactics to different organizations, to include our local Chamber of Commerce. Well, slap me silly, because after reading Cami Baker's book *Mingle to Millions*, I realized there is an array of wisdom yet to be learned. I was faced with the cold hard facts of my networking shortcomings and enlightened to extraordinary networking strategies. Or, what Cami Baker (and now I), refer to as *NetWebbing* strategies. Although spending my many years networking, I must admit, I hated it. Cami Baker has not only enlightened me; but, has also opened my eyes to how much more strategic and fun, NetWebbing truly is. Lastly, I love her "Raw, Real, Relatable" material she shares."

Elena Rahrig
Founder, Transform
www.TransformMastermind.com

"Mingle to Millions is a roadmap to developing the right mindset, in order to build solid relationships with others. Cami, not only, talks about the process of building relationships—she lives it. Cami and her work, clearly walk people through the process of implementing all the right actions at the right time. Don't even think twice about picking this book up, wrapping your mind around it, and sharing it with others. Then, call Cami to tell her I say "Hello." She loves meeting new people and would love to hear from you!"

Ron Sukenick
RonSukenick.com
Public Speaker, Trainer, and Coach
Best Selling Author - Relationship Strategies & LinkedIn Evangelist
National Expansion team for the Gold Star Referral Clubs

"Networking wastes time with random activity; NetWebbing leverages time through planned strategy."

- Cami Baker

MINGLE TO MILLIONS
The Art and Science of Building Business
Relationships and Mastering Referrals.

CAMI BAKER

**TRANSFORM
PUBLISHING**

Mingle to Millions
The Art and Science of Building Business Relationships and Mastering Referrals.

Published by:
Transform Publishing
(567) 259-6454

Cami Baker
Telephone: (603) 785-2598
Email: Cami@CamiBaker.com
www.CamiBaker.com

ISBN: 978-0-692-83910-2
Cover Design: Elena Rahrig
Development Editor: Elena Rahrig
Interior Book Layout: Elena Rahrig

Printed in the United States of America
Second Edition

CONTENTS

FOREWORD

Cami Baker is the genius mind we have all been waiting for. Full of energy, realness, and a relatable aura, Cami Baker squashes what we thought we knew about networking. Just like she states in this book, *the more I know…the more I know I don't know…and the more I know I need to know.*

For years, networking has haunted the likes of many. The dreaded handshakes, fake smiles, all about me attitudes, and energy nowhere to be found. Stuffy business men and women wrapped neatly in their business suits, pretending as though they have it all together. All the while, everyone is wishing they were somewhere else, and are racking their brain to make sense of it all. Hey, I understand, I too, have been there.

Well, not anymore! Cami Baker marches to the beat of her own drum. For some, that may be scary, but for people like me, she is what I have been waiting for. Someone with a vision and a passion to solve a problem, that is in desperate need of being solved. Cami Baker has taken what we have originally been taught and flipped it on its backside. Transforming the dreaded networking to creating a NetWeb.

That's right my friend, Cami teaches us how to rid ourselves of the life sucking networking tactics. She brings innovative and enthusiastic techniques that are sure to gear you straight to elevated success.

Forget the thirty-second elevator speech, the stack of business cards and your tight gripped handshake; because it has been proven, time and again, not to work. This book is not your typical book that you read and walk away from. I encourage you to read, and then take action. What Cami Baker teaches is creating success for people like you and me, from all around the world.

Elena Rahrig
9x Author, 9x Academy Developer, 4x Program Developer
TransformMastermind.com

WHAT IS NETWEBBING?

Is your networking not working as great as you would like? In this book, you will see that I encourage you to stop networking, and instead create a NetWeb for net profit!

Networking does not work; because, in general, it is random activity. People are often taught networking techniques, that simply don't work. In the end, many suck at it; yet, they don't mean to. It's simply that, many are great at building relationships with friends and family; but, when it comes to business it seems icky, weird, awkward, and uncomfortable.

People network without question, because they are told it's what they should be doing. Those who despise it force themselves to do it, and oftentimes, those who actually enjoy it don't fully understand, there is an art and science to building business relationships and mastering referrals.

This is where creating a NetWeb comes in. NetWebbing is strategic, and a sophisticated way to set your intention through your mindset and actions, before an event. This then allows for you to pay attention to your actions, and the reactions of others during the event. Once you learn to effectively pay attention, you will create retention of the resources, relationships, and revenue that you truly desire.

The three pillars of this philosophy are: Intention, Attention, and Retention. To get a true understanding of the NetWebbing concept, we will go through each of these many times during the book. Just know, if you are introverted, it's okay—I am also introverted at my core. Being extroverted is a learned skill. Trust me, if I can do it, anyone can do it! You will see from my story, that anyone can become skilled at the art and science of building relationships and mastering referrals.

In this book, you will learn, in detail, about networking sharks, and how they show up to events looking for their next victim to prey on. Also, you will learn about the skunks who spray their business cards out to everyone, and then pray someone hires them. Then you will learn about the squirrels, who collect business cards and then stash them away just in case they need them someday. You will see that, you more than likely, have been networking as a shark, a squirrel, and a skunk; but, I will teach you the wise ways of the spider through netwebbing. As you grow to understand netwebbing, and utilize the strategies, you will find that netwebbing is, not only fun, but, is also strategic, producing you the results you truly desire.

With NetWebbing, you are creating a synergy and a web of resources, relationships, and revenue through the strategies of the three pillars intention, attention, and retention. When a spider creates a web, she is strategic, she is smart, and she is sophisticated in her planning. She knows where to position herself to attract what she wants. She knows where to start each strand of her web, how to intertwine each connecting part so they are strong, and she knows why she is doing it. And when her masterfully created web is completed, she simply sits back, relaxes, and waits for what she wants to come to her. She puts forth much effort to create her web; yet, because, it is well thought out, both in placement and structure, once created, she simply maintains its connectivity and reaps the rewards of her efforts.

No matter what your thoughts were of a spider before this analogy, I invite you to look at the elegant, sophisticated, strategic, beautiful, and masterful way she works her magic. I encourage you to ask yourself: *Have I been acting as a shark, skunk, squirrel, or spider?* More than likely, you have been acting as at least one of the four, or a combination of the first three. If you have not started networking at all yet, then be excited for what you are about to learn that will get you started on the right track. The bottom-line is, you have the choice of who you want to be seen as, and how you want to be received and perceived in your marketplace. If you have been acting as a shark, skunk, or squirrel, don't worry—I have personally have been a shark, a skunk, and a squirrel at one time in my life (and sometimes all three at once).

I am not proud of the relationships that I have ruined, never made at all, and the relationships that I never had the chance of taking to a higher level because of my *sharkiness*; but, I also don't regret any of it. These experiences created my journey of growth, learning, and studying myself and others. As a result of my experiences at thousands of networking events: spraying and collecting cards, giving God forsaken thirty-second elevator pitches, and ultimately having the blessing of mentoring thousands of one-on-one clients and others from stages worldwide, I have figured out what works and what doesn't.

I offer to you…NetWebbing…a strategic way to create a web of resources, relationships, and revenue, through intention, attention, and retention. This way, you fully understand the art and science of building business relationships and mastering referrals.

PREFACE TO MY STORY

When I first became a networker (many years ago), I was, what I consider, a brand-new networker. I didn't know where to go, who to talk to, what to say, how to start conversations, how to dress professionally, or how to follow up. I was a card collector, and not a business builder. I had the stacks of cards, and I'm going to guess that you do too.

As a beginner networker, I was really intimidated. I was overwhelmed thinking about going to networking events, because it was work. Right? It created anxiety. I just didn't want to go. If you're a beginner networker and you feel this way, believe me when I tell you, I know how you feel.

Now, there came a point in my networking life where I was a very active networker. Perhaps, you are at this stage, and are too, a very active networker. Maybe you go once, twice, or three times a week. Maybe you're gathering all those cards, and you are a card collector. So, now, you have plenty of leads; but, maybe not as much business as you'd like to have. I too have been in that position before. I was doing a lot of networking, but not getting the benefits of it, that I felt I should have been getting. I was meeting a lot of people and made some friends, but wasn't really making the money that I wanted to.

Or, you may be in the position where I am today. Perhaps, you are a professional networker. Now, a professional networker, from my perspective, is someone who, when they network, they not only build good relationships, but they actually follow up. I like to call it: Communicate, Conversate, and Collaborate to create Impact, Income, and Influence.

I've done years and years of networking, and literally, thousands of events. If it had a business card and a thirty-second elevator pitch as part of the routine, I was there. I've been there at six o'clock in the morning, at noon, late at night, and even when I had to leave my daughter with a babysitter and stay up later than normal. I have sat in rooms with two people, and rooms with 30,000 people. I've even been the one who was the speaker at events; again, some with two people and some with 30,000 people. As I said before, I've done a lot of networking, and over that time, I have found a lot of ways, you and I, can be more efficient and effective; which is why I wrote *Mingle to Millions*. It is my desire to share with you, the art of building better business relationships and mastering referrals.

However, I wasn't always this way. I wasn't always in a place where I was attracting business. I'll teach you later in this book about the difference between sharking a room (which is chasing business and being aggressive), and fishing (one who attracts business). I was not always the person who was attracting business.

CHAPTER 1
MY STORY

My business skills began to be built when I was just eight years old. You see, I was buying gum, just to turn around and sell it to other kids, for a profit. I always had the entrepreneurial spirit. I was always looking to monetize and figure things out. It is for this reason, it now comes naturally to me, to work with people to strategize about their networking, their business, their brand, and how they are being received and perceived, in the marketplace.

As a matter-of-fact, taking you back to the term sharking, even back when I was nine years old, I was loan sharking my brother. He is three years older than me, and was always broke. For some reason, I always had money (even back then. This often had my brother coming to me to borrow money. Call it nine-year-old intuition if you want, but I would take things that mattered to him for collateral. I didn't even know what collateral or loan sharking was, but there I was doing it, at the ripe old age of nine.

I've been business-minded my whole life, and eventually moved on to being a Real Estate Agent and a Subcontractor. In these positions, it was essential to my career to be out networking. However, about sixteen years ago, I found myself living in another part of the country than where I am now. I had a brick and mortar business at the time, which was very different from what I was used to (as networking wasn't part of the game). My business was a restaurant by day and a bar by night. People just came to me; so, the marketing was quite different than what I teach today with business networking.

Now, I would love to tell you that my life was all sunshine and roses. However, life began to happen in ways that I never foresaw coming. My ability to make good choices has been a lifelong journey. For example, when I was thirty, I could hear my maternal clock ticking and thought, *it would be a great idea to have a baby with my party buddy*. We thought having a baby would also bring us together (cray-cray, I know); but, we got off birth control and became pregnant.

When my daughter was born, I was owned a bar in Panama City Beach, Florida; which was not conducive to raising a baby. By the time our precious little girl was four-months old, we had made a collective decision to move from where we resided to where he was from. This is where we would choose to raise our baby girl and establish our family— a chapter in life meant to be glorious.

What I realized about moving to a new part of the country was, many things stay the same, while location is the only major change. Whatever problems one has in one part of the country, they will still have in another part of the country. Yes, I took with me all my loves—my baby girl, her father, our 100-pound black Lab, and a U-Haul truck full of our treasured belongings.

However, a geographical relocation is not a cure-all for

problems; because, changing locations doesn't change the mindset. You see, I also brought with me, my ability to make poor choices and my addictions.

Many times, we see business owners who seem to have it all together. We sit in awe at their accomplishments and prestige. However, what happens within the will of a person (no matter successful or unsuccessful), others cannot see. My poor choices would take me down a path, that nobody would ever desire to find themselves on.

So here I was, in a new part of the country, with a baby who was just a few months old, and not knowing a soul in my city. The father of my child didn't live up to his promises; and I was miserable, broke, a single mother, and starting over.

I succumbed to a J-O-B. Also known as, **Just-O**ver-**B**roke. A business owner turned employee, I found my way to cope with my situation. Needless-to-say, it wasn't the best coping mechanisms, but it sufficed my hunger to fill the void in my soul. Long story short, my new boss became my boyfriend, and my drinking buddy. We began drinking from the time we got up until the time we went to bed. Despite knowing deep within my soul, that I was on a road to self-destruction, it was made clear to me, that being this man's girlfriend was the only way to keep my job. Crazy the life we will live for the sake of making ends meet.

Overall, my actions of pleasing this man, to keep my job, had me feeling like a prostitute. I knew I shouldn't have been doing these things, no matter the consequences; but, before long my life became an addiction. My brain couldn't seem to find another way to function. It is what I knew to do, and so it is (sadly), what I did.

I share my story with you to let you know that I understand—I too have been there. I have hit rock bottom, I have felt defeated, and I know what it feels like to struggle. As I work with people in business, networking, rebranding, and repositioning, I hear all the excuses masked as reasons. Such as: *"Well, Cami, you don't understand my situation."* Or, *"You don't know where I come from"*, *"You don't understand that I'm a single mom, I don't have a lot of money, and I don't know a lot of people."* Or, even, *"I just don't feel very confident or great about myself."* It is essential for you to understand that I can relate. I have not only been there, but I too, have said those exact phrases.

CHAPTER 2
RISING TOWARDS SUCCESS

It was at the time that I made the decision to put down the bottle, put my big girl panties on, and pick my ass up, that life began to happen again; but this time, with great intent. As I ran errands this day, I stopped to pick up the newspaper. For those of you who don't know what a newspaper is, it's the internet in print. In the newspaper, there was an ad for a Research Assistant (I believe that is the proper terminology).

Now, let me tell you about the interview, because it's essential to the story and the lesson. My interview was scheduled for 5:00 p.m., in which I arrived at 4:45 p.m. (being punctual is crucial to one's success). Once there, although I didn't know who he was at the time, Ken, the Broker's right-hand man, offered me a cup of coffee. Being a lover of coffee, I, of course, accepted.

As I sat there, the room began to fill up quickly with others who were there for the same reason as I (fourteen people in fact). Realizing my competition was real, I sat thinking to myself, *Hmm. Why is everyone coming in, and why am I not being called for my interview yet?*

It was a few minutes past five o'clock, when we were all called into a conference room together. It didn't take me long to realize, we were all about to participate in a group interview. The two gentlemen interviewing us, were the Broker at a RE/MAX office and his right-hand-man, Ken. They took turns going around the room, asking each one of us a question. Over time, I realized, their intent was to see who can handle the pressure, and to what degree we could handle it.

Needless-to-say, I don't remember the questions others were asked, but I sure do remember mine. Steve, the broker/owner of the office, looked at me directly while the others watched, and he asked me "Where do you see yourself in three years?" I looked back at him, straight in the eyes, and said, "Working for you."

That was it. That's all I said. That was my interview. I will never forget the day I received the phone call, informing me, I had gotten the job. I was overwhelmed with feelings of being blessed, excited for my new life, and nervous, due to the unknown. Overtime, I found out, I had gotten the job because I was confident and could hold my own in a room filled with competition. Now, please know, I was only about 45 days sober, and I was not feeling as confident as I put off. What got me through, was the power of, *fake it until you make it.*

One of the reasons I got the job, was because Ken was the one who offered me the cup of coffee, and I was the only one, of the 14, who took the cup of coffee. It turned out, he was a big coffee drinker; so, he felt bonded with me. It's funny how the universe gives us what we need, when we need it.

So, I began working for this real estate office as their assistant. I did basically everything a listing agent would do—

except for going on the appointments. I went to the different cities around the area obtaining tax cards, taking pictures of properties, and putting signs up. Also, in the office, I did computer work, looked up phone numbers, created listing packets, and much more. While in the office, I received a lot of mentoring. (Thank God I received mentoring from these folks.) After about a year and a half of working there, I obtained my real estate license, and here's where the fun begins—for me and you.

I'm guessing, you're reading this book because, you want to learn how to create business relationships, that are meaningful and significant. Perhaps, you're wanting to know how to master referrals and have business come to you; instead of having to always chase people. When you learn how to communicate correctly, you can then have memorable conversations; which turns into collaboration. Once you master that, you then can create the impact, income, and influence you truly desire.

When I obtained my license, about a year and a half into working at that office, all-of-a-sudden, I found myself being thrown into the mix to create business. At that time, I still didn't know many people, and I certainly didn't have a center of influence to tap into. As I began attending networking events, I started to realize I didn't know what I was doing. But, I was hungry, tenacious, desperate, and I was in survival mode.

Have you ever gone to networking events, simply because, you know you're supposed to? Everybody tells you, "It's what you're supposed to do." But, somewhere inside, you're not really wanting to be there. You find yourself only going because, you must make this *thing* work. You must prove to your boss that you can do it. You want to move up the leaderboard, and hit the different marks in your office. So, like it or not, you attend networking events.

I was going to networking events early in the morning, in the afternoon, and in the evening. My daughter (at that time), was getting to be three or four years old, and I was leaving her with babysitters, way more than I wanted to. Thank God I was as hungry as I was; because, I went so often that I succeeded, even as much as I had messed up. I can't tell you how many bridges I burned, and how many relationships that I didn't make—all because I was sharkish. I was very aggressive, and it was a real turn off. I would chase people. I would hound and pressure them. I was doing all the things that, I now teach, not to do (and that I often see others do). On top of messing it up at the events, I furthered my mistakes after the event, by not following up. Maybe, my ego got in the way, I didn't know what to say, or I just figured they were going to call me. Truth-be-told, it was a mixture of all three.

I see a lot of people, spraying and praying. They're spraying those business cards everywhere; while assuming other people are going to call them. Let's be honest, how many hundreds or thousands (or tens of thousands), of cards have you given out, and/or gotten back, where nothing else ever happened (other than, maybe, receiving a bulk email, or you got added to somebody's newsletter)? All of this was happening for me; but, little by little, over the years, I thought up many unique and proven ways to create relationships. I realized, being aggressive didn't work. And guess what? There were a lot of books I read, a lot of seminars I went to, and a lot of mentoring and training that I took. I did all of this, so I could learn about other personalities, and understand how I was repelling people.

As I learned about all the things I was doing wrong, I also learned what I could be doing right. As I watched the room at hundreds and thousands of events, I had learned, and have come up with, a system to help you. This system will help you, just like it has helped me. It helps you to build better business relationships and master referrals.

During those early years in my real estate career, I did so much guerrilla marketing—innovative, unconventional, and low-cost marketing techniques aimed at obtaining maximum exposure for a product. Now, as I implement the techniques I know, and helping others to do the same, the amount of lives that have been impacted is astounding. It's time for you to be excited; because, in this book, you are about to learn these same techniques!

Many years ago, I got involved in a network marketing company. Say what you will—good, bad, or indifferent—but, it was network marketing that catapulted my ability to network. I received education from books I was encouraged to read, mentors who I had the blessing of working with, many people who I met, the hundreds and thousands of people on my team, all the conventions that I attended, all the coaching I received, and all the conference calls I listened in on.

Over about a five-year period in that network marketing company, I ended up having 10,000+ national and international people on my team; and I, personally, recruited 131. Now, I don't say that to impress you, but to impress upon you that, 131 recruits is a lot of people. Anyone in network marketing will tell you, the average person can recruit two people, and in my experience, that is just not the case. Have you ever heard the analogy: if you take a penny and double it every day, at day 31, you have over $10 million? If you've ever heard that analogy, then you understand, if every person could bring in two, and they brought in two, and so on, and so on, within two months the entire world population would be involved in network marketing. So, it's just not the case. Having brought in 131 recruits, required having the ability to bridge the humanity gap.

Within the first few weeks of my network marketing career, I had my team growing rapidly. It was during this time, I had people say to me, "Cami, how are you getting people to become your business partner? You meet someone at 8:00 a.m. and by 7:00 p.m., they're in your business. What are you saying to people when you go to events? How are you approaching them?"

What I had learned through this experience was, people didn't know they were just like me—if I could do it, so could they. They struggled because they were acting just like me, as the old Cami—the Cami who once was a shark. You see, they were active networkers who were out doing a lot of networking; but, they weren't really getting the results they wanted to. I even met professionals (people who I worked with, who were in high finance and had high rises in downtown New York City), who also weren't proficient at having a simple conversation with someone, who they had never met before.

As those questions kept coming at me, I began sitting down with one person at a time. We would talk about a good handshake, good eye contact, how to create conversation, how to follow up, and all the simple basic functions of connecting—that really aren't so simple. People often find these to be difficult because, let's face it, we weren't taught this in school. School teaches us certain content that enables us to obtain a certain type of career. I know many kids who graduate, who can't even balance a checkbook, and can't even look people in the eye. It's not that, we as human beings, don't want to have this connection—we just aren't taught how to do it.

After a couple of months sitting down with people, in a one-on-one mentoring situation, I found my business growing, with fifteen to twenty people connecting and collaborating in my home. I remember clearly, on Sunday mornings, we would have 15-25 people in attendance. The street would be lined with cars. People would be sitting on the couches, stools, and even the floor. As a matter-of-fact, the stool I'm sitting on now, is one we used back then. With everyone in my home, we would sip coffee, and I would flip my chart, teaching them the techniques I used to grow my business.

Although I was leading the pack, and doing well, it was throughout these years that I realized, I still had much to learn. You see, I came to realize: *the more I know, the more I know that I don't know, and the more I know that I need to know.* Therefore, I began attending classes to learn about personality styles, neuro linguistic programming (NLP), and how to pause in the right places (so, people want to hear the next words I was about to speak). There were all these techniques, that I went so long in life not knowing. I realized, it's about learning human nature, and how we all respond.

Once I had launched, what I call, my living room team, I then began hosting conference calls. I found the conference calls to be beneficial to my network's growth, as I moved from New Hampshire to Massachusetts and then to New York City. Conference calls made global business easy. However, in each new location, I was set back to not knowing anyone personally. This meant, it was time to recruit, communicate, and continue business.

My first step in business, after settling into a new location, was to reach out to different meetup groups and entrepreneur groups. Also, I would create my own events; which by the way, we will talk about a little bit later in this book, during the topic: *Be the Event*.

CHAPTER 3
INTROVERT TO EXTROVERT

Are you between eighteen and eighty? Are you male or female? Are you a business owner, or would you like to be a business owner? Are you independently wealthy, or well on your way? Are you educated, or are you a high school dropout?

What I have found is, your answers don't matter. It doesn't matter where you are from—from the Backroads of Maine to Broadway in New York City, or the Hills of Tennessee to the Beaches of California, and anywhere in between—human beings are human beings. The dreams we have and the fears we have, are all the same.

When I created the *Mingle to Millions* brand, I decided to use it to our advantage—not to take advantage, but to have the advantage. Understand, the people around you are not as great at networking as you think they are. Sometimes, you may feel, when you walk into a venue, everyone there knows what they're doing—*Everyone gets it, but me. Everyone's having a great time, except for me. Everyone else knows how to create conversation. Everyone else feels comfortable in their own skin.* The fact is, the majority, feel just like you (and how I used to).

Many believe that I am an extrovert. However, the truth is, I'm not. Some of my contemporaries, who teach networking, are extroverts. As a matter-of-fact, I was interviewed recently by Emily Utter who said to me, "Cami, since we are extroverts," and she continued with her statement. I, at the end of it, said to her, "Emily, I want to back up a second, and correct one thing. I'm not an extrovert. I'm actually quite introverted."

For the people who I share my wisdom with, I feel it is important for me, as a coach, a mentor, a trainer, and an author in this genre, to let them know that I am not an extrovert. For me, learning how to create a NetWeb is not a talent—it doesn't come natural to me; rather, it is a skill—something that I practiced and got better at over time. When an introvert acts like an extrovert, they learn to turn on an extrovert personality when need be. Therefore, if you are naturally an introvert, don't worry—you can learn. To learn how to NetWeb, is simply to learn how to talk to people. However, in all actuality, you're not really learning how to talk to people; rather, you're remembering how to.

Through the process of practicing being an extrovert, you become reminded of all the things you naturally know, innately as a human being. You can learn (or be reminded of), how to bridge the humanity gap, how to make a great first impression, and how to create conversations. As you learn how to have conversations, you then begin to collaborate to create impact, income, and influence.

As this book progresses, I'm going to address the questions, comments, and misconceptions, that I hear over-and-over again, in different situations. By the end of this book, you will have great insights to what I know and apply. You'll gain full understanding to what creates your success, and what hinders your success. All-in-all, I want you to begin to focus on quality, not quantity. Focus on upping your game and focus on being the game.

Before we move on, I want to congratulate you for jumping on this journey with me to Mingle to Millions. Mingle to Millions can mean millions of dollars for you. It can mean, millions of people who see you in a movie, who read your book, or whose lives are changed, all because, you helped with something that you're passionate about. Mingle to Millions can mean millions in whatever genre that is for you. For me, Mingle to Millions means, millions of people will not only read this book, but will also receive and implement the information, and then take it out into the marketplace.

PART 1
QUESTIONS

CHAPTER 4
HOW DO I FIND EVENTS?

What is typical? Typical networking is all the places you know, like, and trust. Well, you may know and trust, but, like. that could be questionable. These places are your local networking platforms: The Chamber of Commerce, BNI, Women Networking Groups, etc. It is my understanding, you are reading this book because you need more, and more importantly, you want more. In other words, you're not getting everything you truly desire out of these groups; whether it be, enjoyment or more business—you're not getting it. This is why, I want to encourage you to open your eyes to all the opportunity around you. Think outside of the norm—what you're accustomed to. Throughout this book, I have taught you, and am going to continue to teach you, how to make these platforms work better for you. However, it is evenly important to begin to recognize the many other platforms out there for you to take advantage of, that you more than likely, currently are not.

Before we dive into the many platforms, I want to encourage you to stop thinking about networking as a place you go to, or something you put on your schedule. Networking is all around you. Networking is simply, opportunity. It is not brick and mortar. When you begin to see networking as opportunity, instead of something you must go to and brick and mortar, you will begin to gain more understanding as to why I call it NetWebbing and not netWORKing—it becomes strategic, and not a waste of time.

Let's take my friend John, for example. John asked me, "Where do I go to network?" This was fascinating that he had asked me this, because John has a multimillion dollar company; which means he is an intelligent business man. How does a smart businessman not know where to go? With all his resources, he is still just like the masses—not certain where to go and how to network. My reply to him was, "John, you can network anywhere. You can even go to a yacht club and network." Throwing that example out of thin air, ended up being the perfect example for John to relate to. He responded with, "I love boats. I go to yacht clubs all the time. I just never thought about networking while I was there. I usually sit by myself."

As I keep in touch with John, I know he is utilizing his normal establishments for networking—something many don't do. He now sits at the bar and engages with the other members, instead of by himself. Instead of looking for Chamber of Commerce events and other organizational events, he created his own events where he already is, and already enjoys being. Furthermore, for his statute, this is perfect for him. The majority of Chamber of Commerce members, don't have multimillion dollar businesses in manufacturing; therefore, they are not John's target audience. Yet, the yacht club, golf clubs, and clubs of these sorts, are exactly where he needs to be—they possess John's target audience.

So, the questions that remain are: What type of people are you networking with? Are you networking with whoever is thrown in your path? Whoever just happened to join the same networking group as you? Or, are you intentionally choosing the people you need to be networking with? Who you are networking with, will help you think of what platform you should be using to network. For example, if you want to reach people from around the world, then online would be your platform to begin with (keeping in mind you will want to search out physical gatherings of like-minded people on a global level. Mastermind groups are becoming more popular as time goes on. This is because they allow you to connect with people all around the globe. Furthermore, it allows you to pick the group that resembles your own mindset. You can see if the group is filled with amateurs or filled with successful men and women who are where you're currently at, or where you want to get to. The mindset of the people you choose to network with, should be your number one priority when networking.

Let's take Vistage for example. Vistage is a group that contains CEOs of one million dollars or more in annual revenue. The Vistage group that I am speaking about, contains CEOs whose annual revenue is between one million and one hundred million dollars. This is where I met John, who I talked about earlier. He was there taking notes, because he was there to learn. This is exactly why John caught my attention that day. You see, people who are successful have a unique mindset. This mindset is what I call a "growth mindset". They are not rolling out of bed struggling to get through the day, and wondering what life is going to throw at them. Instead, they live by intention. They make their life happen. They understand the power of knowledge, and because of this, they are constant learners. Now, these are just the types of people who I want to create a NetWeb with. People who are like me, who have knowledge to share with me, and who I can share my knowledge with. This then allows us to create a NetWeb together and reach the success we truly desire. My question to you is: Are you networking with people who are stagnant? Who are just trying to close a deal and get through the day? Or, are you creating a NetWeb with like-minded people who you can collaborate with to create the impact, income, and influence that you want to create?

When it comes to creating a NetWeb, understand that you network wherever it is you are at. You can be standing in line at Dunkn' Donuts or the gas station. When someone appears to be just the type of person you desire to connect with, reach out and conversate. However, I do find it important to share with you even more platforms that are available to you. Have you ever heard of MeetUp.com? Well, if not, I strongly encourage you to check it out. Meetup.com is an online social networking portal, that facilitates offline group meetings in various localities around the world. Meetup allows members to find and join groups unified by a common interest; such as: politics, books, games, movies, health, pets, careers, or hobbies.

The meetups that you will find at meetup.com, are a great way to turn your netWORKing into NetWebbing. You can attend an array of events. If you like to walk dogs, take a bike ride, or like to decorate, here is where you will find exactly what you are looking for. Now, those mentioned are just examples, you may not be interested in any of those; but, you hopefully get my point. The point is, find meetups that share a common interest with you, and possess like-minded people.

Connecting through common interest is a great way to break the ice and feel comfortable faster. Lastly, attending fun meetups, breaks the monotony of the typical networking events that many of us are bored with.

Another platform for you to consider networking on, are expos. I have attended hundreds of expos and have found great value in them. Any large town in the U.S.A. holds expos. For example, the town that I currently live in, has an expo center. Any given week, at least twice or three times a month, there's an expo; whether it's the Reptile Expo, Bridal Expo, or the Tri-County Business Expo. Everyone who has a booth at an expo is in business, and they are looking to create a NetWeb, to communicate to collaborate, to create impact, income, and influence…just like you.

In summary, I encourage you to search what is going on in the area, where you would have fun creating your NetWeb. Look up expos, tradeshows, seminars, and fundraiser events. Don't always stay local, attend free events, or events that are just convenient. Begin your search with regional events, and then expand to a national and global search. Some of the best events are found by asking questions at the event you're at. Instead of asking: *What do you do?*, ask: *What other events do you know of, that are coming up?* Lastly, the number one way to create your NetWeb is to Be the Event.

RECAP:
1 You can create a NetWeb anywhere you are.
2 Know who it is you should be creating your NetWeb with.
3 NetWeb with like-minded people.
4 Utilize Meetup.com.

5. Attend expos, tradeshows, seminars, and fundraiser events.
6. Don't stay just stay local. Search national and global events.

CHAPTER 5
WHAT DO YOU MEAN
BE THE EVENT?

This topic is one of my favorites to teach. Also, it's a program that I work diligently on with my clients. Let's first discuss, what types of questions you would ask, if you knew what I know. With over fifteen years of experience in the business world—in the public eye—thousands of events attended, hosted, and spoken at, and the tens of thousands of people I've met, spoken with, and worked with...I must know something. Right?

One aspect of being the event, is looking at it from the perspective of doing fundraisers or raising community awareness. Being the event is especially powerful for people who want to speak, be heard, impact many with a message, or someone whose goal is to attract clients (as opposed to chasing them).

There are several ways you can, *be the event.* First-of-all, when you go to an event that someone else is hosting, you can *be the event* from the perspective of having a major mindset shift. With a mindset shift, you decide to walk into that room feeling comfortable in your skin, confident, and knowing what you have is what people need, want, and deserve. When you have this type of posture at an event, you are being the event—creating a situation where people can receive you as the professional they need.

Let's take *being the event* to an even bigger level. Most people who attend events simply sit in the room amongst the people, mingle, and hand out business cards. While those who are *being the event,* know and understand the importance of, not just mingling, but also following up. If you truly desire to *Mingle to Millions,* the mingle and the follow-up is a great place for you to start. As a matter-of-fact, that's where we must start.

Over time, it became clear to me that I could be the event, the speaker, and position myself as an expert. Whatever topic you use to position yourself as the expert, you must understand that you, are in fact, the edified expert. If you are like I was, and don't fully grasp the concept of the term *edified expert*, allow me to explain.

To edify someone simply means to raise them up—to raise them up in the eyes of another. Perhaps you are more familiar with the term *elevate*. Elevate also means to raise up. Just think of an elevator that takes you to the top of a skyscraper. As an edified expert, you take people to the top of their own personal skyscraper of success.

Whether you are talking highly about someone who you plan to connect to another, someone is talking highly about you, or you are being introduced to a large audience before taking the stage, you are in an edified position of authority and expertise. People will see you differently, receive you differently, and treat you differently. Think about how you would feel, and the thoughts that would enter your mind, in the moments of meeting a celebrity. Your posture and demeanor would change, and your eyes would even have a different ray of light in them. I have seen it thousands of times. These changes within people, happen because they have mentally edified the person.

When I was in network marketing, we were taught to implement edification at all events. The process includes being authentic and sincere when speaking highly about an individual. Once we edified the chosen person, we then would bring them into the conversation to make the connection. This created starry-eyes and words of excitement, such as, "Really? I'm honored!" This is exactly how we should be making people feel, in all channels of life. We should be raising people up, by speaking highly of them and connecting them to the right people—the people who will help them be successful in both, their personal and business adventures.

As a matter-of-fact, I am constantly sharing this with my clients. When you're going to introduce two people, because you think this person should be referred or introduced, there's a level of, "Oh, hey Bob. Here's Mary's number. You should call her." Or, "Hey, Bob. I told Mary to call you." What you want to do instead is, send an email or Facebook message to both parties, or introduce them at a live event (while complimenting them), so they're excited to work together.

When in the position to create a NetWeb, as a keynote speaker, I am always in and netwebbing mode. Especially when I am in a new area, where I don't know anyone. This is a great time to research, reach out and relationship build, in order to find where the local chamber meetings are being held, along with other networking groups, entrepreneurial groups, and meet-ups. However, it's important to use the right language, right wording, and even more importantly the right how—how to use the right words and positioning.

The right language is simply being engaging and friendly; while making sure the person knows it is personal. For you to make it personal, you simply direct your attention to them—their accomplishments, how you can help them, or what the two of you have in common. For example, "I'm very impressed with your headshot. Who did that for you? I would love for them to do mine." An even more elaborate example for you is the following letter I sent a meeting planner:

Hi _____!

The reason I am contacting you is because I have been invited to speak at a large networking event in Ohio. Since I will be in your area, I am reaching out to you to see if you would like me to share some strategic NetWebbing tips with your group? I trademarked NetWebbing, because networking is an activity that wastes time. Meanwhile, NetWebbing is a strategy that leverages time masterfully.

Please see the attached list of groups I have supported over the years, which includes companies such as: Berkshire Hathaway, Microsoft, and Century 21. You will also notice, I have had the honor of being on HGTV's House Hunters, in Success from Home Magazine, and was a judge on The Celebrity Apprentice. I share this fun list with you because, since I can accomplish this through creating a NetWeb, I know you and your people can do big things too!

Let's chat this week to see how I would be a good fit for your group. Feel free to watch these videos of my work and let's talk on Tuesday at 4pm, or is Friday at noon better for you?

Cami Baker
CamiBaker.com

***Notice the choice of words, and how I *assumed the sale* and created my credibility; but, was humble about it.

Some of this language would include your bio, your body of work, and/or your speaker packet. We all have credentials we can use to our advantage. Sometimes it takes working with another person, to search out how to position these credentials. When I work with a client, I help them create their speaker packet, and help them to notice there are many groups, individuals, and companies who they have worked with that they can include. For example, in my case I have worked with many people whose names you would not recognize; however, here is an example of their credentials I can use to my advantage, to show my level of expertise.

When you are researching, reaching out, and relationship building, your email or phone call to these leaders should be friendly, upbeat, positive, and the *assume the sale* type language. Below is another example for you.

"Hi Mike! I love the name of your group *Entrepreneurs on Fire!* That is in true alignment with who I am and how I do business! As a matter-of-fact, not only am I also an entrepreneur who is on fire, I work with international authors, life coaches, franchise owners, non-profits, and fortune 500 companies, such as: Berkshire Hathaway and Ronald McDonald House. I share with them how to strategize their business networking, so they are positioned in the marketplace to attract clients and build credibility in the marketplace.

I would love to get on the phone and discuss a collaboration, to not only attend one of your gatherings of like-minded individuals, but to also, share from the stage, how building business relationships can land them in all kinds of media, and gain free exposure to increase their referral business. I have availability on Tuesday and Friday this week. Which is better for you?"

In other words, I promote my skills through a bit of an example. I offer to share what can benefit them, and at the end, I give him a call to action with a choice of two options. Never ask a "yes or no" question; because, if they say "No" there is no going back. Don't ask an open-ended question when scheduling an appointment, as you want them to set the appointment. He may say Tuesday or Friday doesn't work, but now we are in a conversation, and I can ask if morning or afternoon is better on a different specified day that week.

For me, when I speak at events, my specialty is on creating a NetWeb—for you it may be about something else. Perhaps, for you, it's about financial responsibility, a home buyer seminar, how to use better lighting and photography equipment, make-up application, being an advocate for the Make a Wish Foundation, or even global warming.

Whichever reason you find that you are *being the event,* it is important to know how to present the package of the product. For me, as a speaker, the product is myself. I must position myself as an expert on my topic when I speak with people at events—just like you should. Also, I need to let them know that I am available and eager to educate, inspire, and impact the people in their community. When at events, you won't find me eager to collect business cards from people. Instead, as I position myself as an expert, people are eager to shake my hand and give me their business cards without my asking. What I see is, most people just hang out and collect cards, with no intention to follow-up. I have done that thousands of times, and this is how I know it doesn't work.

To win in business, you must be able to position yourself as an expert. When you do, you will find that people become attracted to you—instead of you chasing people down for their business card. Perception is everything. You may not feel like an expert. You may feel mediocre in your industry. However, you are in fact an expert at the level of expertise you are currently at. Especially to someone who knows little about what you teach—to them, you are an expert. So, I encourage you to begin seeing yourself as the expert you are, and then position yourself as such.

Perception of reality is tangible. Perhaps, tangible in the minds of people; but, in any manner, it is tangible. Perception truly is reality. So, my question to you is, how are people perceiving you? Are they perceiving you as just another bozo on the bus? Or, are they perceiving you as a powerful example, who they would like to follow, employ, or strategize with?

When you have fifteen to sixty minutes to get on a stage and share with people what you do, how you do it, why you do it, and who you do it for, they'll want more. If you find yourself not sure how to deliver your message, know that your overall goal is to share tips of how to do something better. When you help others take what they are already doing, and teach them how to do it better, you are taking years of trial and error off of people's business growth. You are giving them the exact *how to,* in order to keep them from having to *figure it out* on their own. Now, when you are nearing the end of your speech, be sure you have an offer. Let's face it, as an expert, you need to be getting paid, and you deserve to be paid. Just know, when you speak you attract those who want to do business with you. To be on stage is to be the event.

When you are *being the event,* you have a new way to market yourself. You could be creating a fundraiser, a party, a community awareness activity, or even an auction. (I've done those before too.) For example, one series of events that I've done in the past are antique car shows. I had a 1964 Mustang, and because I had that car, I ended up doing an antique car show for a local venue for seven years in a row. Turns out, now I'm an expert at coordinating antique car shows. What I figured out in this seven years, was hosting an event gave me several months to use the event to market, promote, and position myself differently.

These car shows gave me a reason to talk to people. Here's the beauty of putting on an event that's a few months out. I had a flyer and would go into businesses asking them if they would promote the car show for me. I wasn't walking in with business cards, a briefcase, or looking official. I had hundreds of people who I got to meet just by walking down Main Street, U.S.A. However, it didn't stop there. I was also able to expand my territory by reaching out to the town next to Main Street, U.S.A. Passing flyers out on a beautiful day is a great way to get out, enjoy the day, enjoy some sunshine, meet peop e, and do some real NetWebbing. It is much better than sittin g in a stuffy conference room for an hour and passing out a bu ch of business cards to people who are never going to call t e. What a waste of time that can be!

So, I'm out with my flyers, enjoying the day. and I say, "He\, listen. I have this flyer. Proceeds go to the Live and Let Live Farm. It's about an antique car show. Do you mind if we put in your window?" Because of that, some people said "Sur , put it in the window!" some people said, "No, we can't do th it." and for some people, it created conversation. I'd have a nic five or ten-minute chitchat with those people, and I had a wa of being able to follow-up with them. I would say to them "Do you have a business card? What I can do next time is, se d you an email with the flyer, let you know how many peop e came to the car show, and how much money we raise ." In other words, I set-up the follow-up right then, and there

There is a strategy in how we build our business relati nships and master referrals. It's not just about spraying our itch and cards while praying for business, showing up at an e\ent late, leaving early, and pretending that we did some netw rking. When you're being the event, there are many piec that play into it.

Now, there are times when I have an idea for an event; but, don't have a venue. So, before I can do the event, it's my job, o go out and vet venues. I'll put together a list of ten poss le venues that hold 100-500 people. Once I have some venu s to vet, I then go and talk about the event to the people at th se venues. This gives me a reason to get out and mingle in a uch more creative and fun way. If the first venue and the first person I talk to is perfect, I still go and talk to all ten; because, the point of it, isn't just to find the venue, it's also to have a reason to talk to people.

When holding an event, be sure to include a cause. For example, you can use your event as a fundraiser for an organization, such as, the American Red Cross or The Humane Society. Just keep it away from religion or politics, and keep it on young people, older people, animals, or veterans. In doing so, you can't lose. When you include an organization in your event, you now get to bring in more money for the cause, and you have the organization to help you get butts in seats and share their resources. Overall, it becomes more exciting, and you show people a piece of your heart by caring for others.

When I was in New York and New Jersey, I would do events where I would be a speaker. I would say, "Listen, I personally don't want any money for my speaking time. However, let's do this. Let's take twenty or thirty dollars at the door, and let's donate it to the Ronald McDonald House, or let's donate it to the American Cancer Society," The key to picking an organization to give back to, when you are the speaker at someone else's event, is to pick a cause that the meeting planner is passionate about. This way, the organizer is even more passionate about you being a part of the event and the event itself. Moreover, people are much more likely to come to the event because, not only is it great content, but it's also going to benefit this organization. This style of NetWebbing is much bigger than standing in a networking event handing out a card or getting on a stage to talk to people. You can make these events as big, as yummy, and as productive and powerful as you want to make them.

Consider this. If you are wanting to host a community even to bring awareness to the homeless in your community, here' what I did. I have a friend who lives in Australia, who is psyc ic and can do a John Edwards impersonation. He's passi nate about the homeless folks in his area, and needs to get k own better in the community that he lives in. So, I said to hi n, "James, here is what we're going to do. We're going to have you do the John Edwards impersonation. You will need a ve ue that holds at least 100 people. Now, we can schedule this few months out, and make it a fun event that people want to cc me to. However, you must find the venue. Finding the venu gives you a reason to go out and talk to everyone in the com unity, about finding a venue big enough to hold 100 peop e. Once you have the venue, you can go to all the busi esses, and you can promote the event. You can even do little 30 to 45-minute meet and greets at different offices for free. This will lead them to come to your event.

An event like this can turn into something big. When I talk bout you becoming local, regional, national, or global, this is hu e for that. If you're a local person, and you want to help the l cal school system, you can do an event that brings all the child en. I've done local events when I was with RE/MAX as a rea estate agent. The RE/MAX agents have the big hot air ballo n at their disposal to use, at no cost to them. All they must do, is guaranteed to get media and a certain amount of peop e there. I say "all they must do" with my tongue in my chee because there's a lot to it. When you're focused, when you' thinking big, when you're expanding your comfort zone, and hen you're wanting to be the event, have something like a ho air balloon come.

I had it come a couple of times, and all-of-a-sudden

now the mayor is there, and the newspaper is there. We had a thousand kids on a football field taking pictures, the RE/MAX hot air balloon going up, free media publicity, and the CamiBaker.com team waving at the camera with big grins on their faces!

There are many different manners in which you can be the event. I'm telling you, when I had the hot air balloon come into the area, there was lots to talk about, and lots of publicity and promotion. Free stories were written about me, RE/MAX, and the school. If you're passionate about schools, the kids, and the elderly in the area, then you can do events locally that benefit them. Don't pay for advertising. Instead, get a story written about you. People don't care about a 50% off coupon in the paper. They care about a story that entails a local business person, who is doing something to give back to the community. That's what they want to read about. That's what gets on the news.

You can also do this on a regional level. As a matter-of-fact, same concept: RE/MAX and hot air balloon. In my local area, there were local kids who were living in situations that were not very good. We had the hot air balloon come to a Boys & Girls Club that was more of a regional level. The balloon came, and we ended up putting together an entire event around it. We had face painting, dancing, and karate demonstrations. Different vendors, the title companies, and the mortgage businesses got involved. I can't even tell you, how many hundreds of people I met by doing this regional event.

Do you want to save the whales? Do you want to save the trees? Do you want to get seen on a national level? I have people who I work with that do Make-A-Wish Foundation events, so they can be seen on a national level. *Be the event.* When you be the event you are edified, and you are the expert. It gives you so many things to talk about besides yourself, and the boring thirty-second elevator pitch that you've been practicing.

It expands how people see you. It gives you something to look forward to. It gives you a way to have a win-win-win. Now your networking, or NetWebbing, isn't about you. It's about the people who you're going to benefit, and the hundreds of people who you'll meet leading up to the event—that you wouldn't have met if you hadn't held the event.

As you can see, there are multiple reasons for being the event. When I put together an event in my area where, we're going to have a few hours of public speakers and motivational speakers, it gives me a reason to reach out, mingle, and collaborate with people who do very similar things to what I do.

CHAPTER 6
WHY DON'T PEOPLE RESPOND TO ME?

"What do you do?" "Hey, what do you do?" "What do you do?" "What do you do?" "What do you do?" "What do you do?" Do you ever feel people have nothing to say other than, "What do you do?" Realistically, who gives a shit about what you do? Right? *What do you do?* is like the most boring question you can possibly ask someone; yet, that's all people can think to ask. Asking the question *What do you do?* is one example of, what I refer to as, sharking. It looks like this, "Hey, what do you do?" Then they look around the room like they really don't care, and they are looking for their next person to ask: "What do you do?"

When you ask: *What do you do?* you are pigeon-holing the person. Don't you do more than one thing? Don't you do a lot of things? Most people have a job, and a business on the side. People have a business, and are entrepreneurs; while creating a product, or inventing something. Furthermore, most people volunteer, and have something going on that they are very passionate about. Frankly, for me, I don't care what somebody does; rather I care what they're passionate about.

What people do is not nearly as important to me as why they do it, how they do it, or who they do it for. When I go to an event, I would much rather walk up to someone and say, "Hey, what project are you working on right now?" Another format to ask this same question is: "Hey, tell me something about you, that has nothing to do with what you do for work, or where you're from." When you say it this way, people are often caught off guard; because, they are waiting for you to ask, "What do you do?" They are waiting to deliver to you, their boring thirty-second elevator pitch.

As you catch them off guard, you are truly snapping them out of their zone. I saw Anthony Robbins on a video recently called, *I Am Not Your Guru*. He talks about why he uses the F bomb, "I can drop the F bomb quickly and somebody will say, *Wow, that language is...*" He said, "It helps people snap out of the monotone state of not thinking and brings them into the moment."

By asking someone, what project they are working on, you do the same thing. When I say to someone, "What are you working on right now?" it causes them to look around and look up. When people look up they are thinking. When they are thinking, they are engaged. Moreover, it shows that you truly do care about what they are interested in; to the point they get a little grin on their face, and then they share with you what is truly important to them—what they are passionate about. So, you see, as a business networking strategist and positioning expert, there is a deeper level to all my madness!

I want you to picture yourself in the situation of asking someone: *What do you do?* Now, hear their response: *I sell insurance.* Okay, great, they sell insurance. What is your response to that? Where is the conversation that transpires into collaboration? Truly, there is none, or very little. Now, picture yourself in a situation where you ask someone: *What project are you currently working on?* Now, hear their response: *I'm putting together an event, and I have many speakers who are coming. Currently, we are looking for a venue.* Or, *I'm writing a book and I'm really excited about it because it's a romance novel. It's about my first boyfriend.* What is your response to those statements? I'm sure you can think of many natural responses that leads to conversation and collaboration. Remember, ask questions that lead to conversation and collaboration to create impact, income, and influence.

Listen, I get it, there is a time and a place for everything. There may even be a time and a place to ask *What do you do?* I'm just inviting you, and suggesting to you, to be bold and different. It's important to realize, the number one thing people love to talk about is, themselves. When we ask someone about their current project, it opens the door for them to do just that. They then, walk away from the conversation feeling great about themselves, and about you— they like you; and all you did was given them a platform to talk about themselves.

Furthermore, you can quickly learn a lot about a person based on what they're passionate about. Do they read, write, play in a band, garden, or even dog sit? If they read, this can lead into knowing what types of books they read, and why they enjoy these types of books. Are they reading *Think and Grow Rich,* or, a Stephen King novel? Once, you discover this, you discover more about their personality and what trips their trigger.

If you are wondering why people are shying away from you, it could be because, they see what I see—a shark. A shark is easy to sniff out. I can feel when I am in the presence of a shark, and I can visually see it in the person's eyes. Their eyes glaze over, they lean in, and within seconds of realizing I'm not their target audience, their eyes go dead as they begin to think of someone else they'd rather be talking to. Then they lose eye contact all together, as they prepare themselves to swim away. Now, being who I am, I speak up when I see this happen. For example, I was at an event, and a gentleman totally sharked me. I looked at him and said, "Oh no you didn't! You did not just glaze over and totally dismiss me. Did you just dismiss me because of how I answered your question?"

The point is, notice how you are being received. Not everyone is going to be conscious of sharking; however, subconsciously, everyone is. So, if you are sharking, know, people are sensing it— even if they aren't like me, and instead choose not to say something to you about it.

Have you ever noticed a person in the same room as you (at the same event), who you can see from across the room, and who you haven't talked to yet; but, there is something unique about them that peaks your interest enough to desire to talk to them? Or, same scenario, but, you just don't like the person. Again, you've never met them, never spoken to them, but, there's just something about them that rubs you the wrong way. Hey, we have all experienced this at one time or another. The reason we feel this way (whether positive or negative), is because of their body language. Each and every one of us, either attracts people or repels people. So, my question to you is: Are you attracting people, or are you repelling people?

Next questions: How are you communicating when you introduce yourself? What first impression are you giving? What do your conversations sound like? Are they meaningful and masterful, or are they boring? You will find your answers to these questions, as you pay attention to how people are responding to you. Do people smile when talking to you? Do they engage in the conversation? Do they lean back from you? Do they look around? All-in-all, are they enjoying the conversation as much as you are, or are you in your own little world, being the only one enjoying the conversation?

There are many ways to engage with people, other than the standard monotonous question of: *What do you do?* I want to know, why they do what they do, who do they do it for, what inspires them, what are they frustrated about, do they have children and a spouse, what problem do they solve, and what problem do they need me to help them solve.

WorldwideNetWeb, is an annual event that I host; sometimes in Boston, and sometimes in other locations around the world. At these events, I post a large round sign that says, "No elevator pitch, and no asking: *What do you do?*" Then during the announcement, I address this rule and inform people that, I ask for a $20 donation to the charity of choice when I hear someone break the rule. I then go on to explain, the reason is because, you are not being original, and you are not creating a Network on Fire. In fact, I even play with people, when I attend an event and they ask me: *What do you do?* I respond with, "I help people stop saying what do you do and learn how to have interesting conversations." Hey, I have to make all the NetWeb creating I do fun too. Right?

Having said that, why are you reading this book? Are

you building a business? Are you wanting to be a better communicator for relationships? More than likely, you are reading this, because you want impact, income, and influence in one form or another. You want resources, relationships, and revenue; and because you want all these things, it's important to take a big step back, take a deep breath, and pay attention to how you are communicating (which begins with non-verbal communication—your body language).

So, when you are ready to be a professional, productive, profitable, and prosperous networker, stop asking: *What do you do?* I'm challenging you to be bold, be daring, and be a maverick—do something different that sets you apart.

PART 2
COMMENTS
AND
MISCONCEPTIONS

CHAPTER 7
DITCH THE PITCH

Dearly beloved, we are gathered here today to put our dear friend to rest. That's right! Someone has died, and that would be the thirty-second elevator pitch. Thank God! Aren't you glad the thirty-second elevator pitch is dead. I know there are networking coaches out there, who are rolling over in their graves screaming, "What? The thirty-second elevator pitch? You had better learn your elevator pitch. You better know how to tell people what you do."

When we utilize an elevator pitch, we assume our product or service can be delivered in a one-size-fits-all package. Wouldn't it be wiser, to showcase your product or service in a light that fits your potential client's needs? Absolutely, it would be! For example, if you were to talk about being a real estate agent, painter, or an insurance salesman, aren't there many ways to offer these services? In the chapter, *What Do You Do?* we talked about this; but, just to bring to your remembrance, I will say it again, "People do more than one thing, and they do it more than one way." You cannot capture all of it in a way that appeals to everyone, in thirty-seconds.

Picture this: You are at an event, someone walks up to you and asks, "What do you do?" Instead, of answering them with your thirty-second elevator pitch, be bold and respond with, "Well, I'm more interested in hearing what it is that you have going on. What projects are you working on?" Or keep it as simple as, "I am an entrepreneur and philanthropist...tell me about you." It's during this time, you can now listen. To listen means to shut your mouth. God gave you two ears and one mouth for a reason. Furthermore, go above-and-beyond listening—pay attention. Pay attention to any frustrations they may talk about; because, frustrations mean there's a problem. As a business person—who solves problems—is the frustrations they are having, a problem that you can solve? If so, you can now respond intelligently to them, by displaying your product and services in a way that they will be interested in listening to you. Ultimately, they are more apt to purchase what it is your selling, without you having to "sell" it.

Think about it. How many times has your elevator pitch served you well? Think about the normal response you receive after you give your dirty thirty. I'm certain it sounds something like this: "Oh, that's interesting. Sounds like you have some great things happening." Then, they begin to give you their dirty thirty, then one of you begins to shark the room (if one of you haven't already begun doing so).

The point is, if you have gone this long torturing yourself, and others, with your dirty thirty, why keep doing it? Move on. Insanity is doing the same thing over and over and getting the same undesired results over and over. Stop being insane. Do something different. Do what I am teaching you. So far, it hasn't failed anyone! Meanwhile, the dirty thirty is failing everyone.

Hey, I get it; whoever came up with the dirty thirty, thought *this sounds good.* Oftentimes, when something sounds good it makes us feel good, so it must be good. How wrong must we be. Just because it sounds good and makes us feel good when we hear the idea, doesn't mean it is good. At some point, we must wise up and give attention to the results we produce. The results of the dirty thirty are dead; therefore, the dirty thirty must die with it.

As a coach, who is also a public speaker and mentor, I help people reach success in a variety of ways, with a variety of techniques. So, if I was to give a dirty thirty, I would be sure to miss an important element of what someone needs help with. Missing a specific element for a key person means, there is no insight as to how I could help the person. In the end, they walk away with a problem that I could have solved, had I taken the time to find out exactly what their problem is, by simply letting them talk.

Picture this: You're at an event, everyone is in a circle, and is taking turns giving their elevator pitch. How many of those people really enlightened you? Made you want to jump up and hire them? Made you eager to not only get their business card, but actually follow-up with them? More than likely this has never happened, or very rarely. Also, look at it from their eyes. How many times has someone been eager to jump up, get your card, and follow-up with you? Hey, I've been there. You leave thinking, *Bob got my card! He's going to hire me!* However, Bob never calls. Yes, in the moment he enjoyed what you said, but, it wasn't powerful enough to push him to follow-up with you.

As a business person, your emotions probably feel like

they are on a rollercoaster ride most days. One moment is good, but then nothing happens. One day is good, but then everything falls apart. I encourage you to stop the madness. Start putting effort into your networking—start making it fun and strategic by creating your NetWeb.

To play with someone, means to share, to go back-and-forth, to give and take, and to pay attention to each other and have fun. When you drop the dirty thirty, and instead, be a NetWeb creator, you begin to conversate—you begin the give and take. Once the give and take occur, you actually, *take something away* from the interaction; whether a sale, a hot lead, a friendship, or a collaboration. Remember, once you reach collaboration you begin to get the impact, income, and influence you truly desire. I promise you, when you drop the dirty thirty, and instead, begin to create your NetWeb the way I'm teaching you, not only will you get to the collaboration portion of the process, but you will get there quicker than you ever thought possible.

I had a client just this week, who did what it is I'm teaching you now. Her name is Terri Foster, and she is a Life Coach, a Fitness Coach, a barrel horse racer, and a CEO and businessperson. She says to me, "Cami, I went to an event yesterday, and there we sat in a circle. The elevator pitches began to fly." She listened to the entire group, and payed attention to their needs. Then, when it was her turn, she knew exactly what she needed to say to reach each person. She did not just give a rehearsed dirty thirty; instead, she tailored her speech, so all would be impacted.

Another great example for you, is my good friend Tammy. She is the Facebook Faucet Queen. We first met in

California, when we both happened to attend the same event, with about 300 people in attendance. There were at least six other people there who offered the same service as Tammy—Facebook ads. Tammy and I were sitting at a VIP luncheon with a group of people, who were all getting to know each other. As extroverted, vivacious, and bubbly as Tammy is, she was still nervous to speak. She didn't know what to say to deliver her message about what services she offers. I said to her, "You know what, Tammy? There's about six people here that do Facebook ads. If somebody asks you: *What do you do?* and you ramble off your thirty-second pitch, about I do Facebook ads, people are going to be thinking, *Wah, wah, wah, wah, wah. You and everybody else.*"

I instead encouraged her by saying, "Why don't you hear about them first, and then, when it's your turn, you can say, for an example, "You know what, Mary? It's great that you're a chiropractor, and that you've been in business for just a couple of years, and you're looking to generate more business. You are exactly the kind of person I like to work with—holistic, you know...active in the community. You're the exact type of client I work with to help generate business. Here's my card. Let me get your information, and let's finish the conversation after the event. Matter of fact let's schedule that now."

By doing what I suggested, Tammy just told Mary, exactly what Mary needs to hear. Instead of a boring dirty thirty, Mary heard that Tammy can help her and is thinking, *Oh, you work with me? You like to focus on holistic people? You like this, that, and the other thing about me? Maybe we can do some business.*

Another tool you can use in place of the dirty thirty

elevator pitch is, a testimonial. For example, when I was a real estate agent, instead of just standing up and saying, "Hi, my name is Cami Baker. I'm a real estate agent. Sure, would love your referrals...blah, blah, blah." I could stand up and say something like this: "My name is Cami Baker and here is what's really cool about what happened this week. I have some clients who are under agreement, and they're moving to Florida. They're already packing their bags and on their way. Why is that exciting? Because, they were on the market twice with two other agents for the last year. I came in, told them exactly what was going on. We were under contract within three days. Now they're on their way to where they want to be, and I'm so happy for them. Cami Baker. I specialize in helping people whose properties have a hard time getting sold."

There are a variety of tools available to you that work—unlike the thirty-second elevator pitch. The most important aspect for you to remember is, let the other person talk first.

For example, as you know by now, I love to be the event—create my own events. When I am at a NetWebbing event, I have something else to talk about besides the great "I AM." For example, when I hosted fundraisers or a community awareness event, I would say something like this: "Hi, everybody. My name is Cami Baker, and I am sponsoring an antique car show for the Live and Let Live Farm. Now the proceeds go to the farm, so I'm looking for people who have antique cars, who love antique cars, who want to be a vendor at the event, who love to give back to the horses, or who may want to volunteer. If that sounds like you, come on over and give me your card."

Okay, so perhaps, to you, that sounded like an elevator pitch. Perhaps, a bit; but I want to make clear to you the difference between your standard elevator pitch, and what I just did. I did not stand up there and say 10,000 "I" statements. I made it all about them. Furthermore, I gave them clear instructions on what I wanted them to do. In all reality, everyone wants to talk about themselves. Nobody really cares about you or what you are selling. Think about it. Do you think people are excited to wake up early, go to a networking event, just hoping to run into you, and hear about what you have to offer? Absolutely not! They are there for the same reason you are— to have people listen to them. So, since you know that is why they are there, do yourself a favor by listening to them and making your speech about them.

When I take the above approach, more times than not, people are intrigued. They respond in such ways as: "Oh, I have antique cars." Or, "I know somebody with three antique cars." Or, "I know that place." "I want to give back." "I want to volunteer." "I'm a Pampered Chef distributor." "I'm a Mary Kay distributor." "I'm a real estate agent." "I want to have a booth." In other words, it creates conversation, and they come over because, they want to learn more about it. In return, it shows me who enjoys giving back, and who I can collaborate with in the future. I'm not standing there giving my thirty-second Cami Baker fame speech. I'm talking about something outside of myself.

The thirty-second elevator pitch is dead; but, let's not be in mourning for too long. Let's celebrate the death of the thirty-second elevator pitch. Let's step powerfully into being able to create conversation that is masterful and meaningful, and gives us a way to follow-up and follow-through, to create the resources, relationships, and the revenue that rock. This way, we can communicate and conversate to collaborate, and create the impact, income, and influence that we all want to achieve. It all starts with ditching the pitch.

CHAPTER 8
NETWORKING ONLINE

Far too often, I hear people say, "But, Cami, I don't need to go to networking events. I do all my marketing online." I can understand this thought process to a certain extent. This is because, people perceive networking as a place they go, or something they put on their calendar. However, with NetWebbing, we are simply communicating with other human beings. As I said before, communication is much more than just our words; and because of this, you cannot fully communicate properly online. When we meet face to face, we now have full communication benefits. We can now see each other's body language, hear their tonality, see their facial expressions, and they in turn, can see ours. This all encompasses: posture, presence, presentation, and perception.

It is for these reasons, that if you are one who prefers to network online, when it is possible, use online platforms that allow you to visually see each other. For example, I love using Zoom.us. Zoom is a simple video conference platform. I'm sure you are familiar with Skype (which is another great platform to use). Zoom is Skype on steroids. With Zoom, you can have hundreds of people in your video conference room. You can see and hear each other—this way body language, facial expressions, and tonality are all able to come into play; allowing you to communicate concisely. Furthermore, you can screen share and record your sessions.

Now, before we get into too much depth on this topic, I first want to make sure you understand the following. First-of-all, I reiterate, networking is not a place you go, or something that you put on your calendar. Networking happens all the time. Also, please know, anytime I use the term network, it's only so you understand what I'm talking about. However, as you begin to see networking in a different light, because of what I am and have been teaching you, I'm sure you will agree with me on the term NetWebbing. I don't know about you, but personally, I don't want to waste time miserably networking. I want to leverage my time masterfully by creating a NetWeb. I don't want to do aimless random activity, I want to be strategic in my planning before, during, and after an event to have maximum results.

Getting back to communicate to conversate, to collaborate to create impact, income, and influence; clear communication and conscious connections are extremely important in today's economy. When you do your business online, there are going to come times when there's an email, a Facebook post, or even a coffee meetup needed. When you're an online marketer, it is even more important for you to go to live local, regional, national, and global events. Simply put, because you're target audience is everywhere—not just in your local area.

When you have a live event to attend, use this time to brush up on your NetWebbing skills. If you are accustomed to doing most of your prospecting, business-building, lead gene ation, and customer contacting online, you are more than likely not going to do very well at a live event—you won't be as pr ductive—which means less results.

I create my NetWeb quite a bit online. A few months ago, received a message from a gentleman on LinkedIn. The more I got to know him, the more I could see he was looking for new salespeople for his firm, new clients, and ways to impr ve his salespeople.

It just so happened, he came across my portfolio. He sent ne a message, and I wrote back to him. (This is part of the communication process.) In my message back to him (inste ad of being dry and professional), I said to him, "I'm sorry for my delayed response. LinkedIn is not something that I'm n every day. If you had sent me a Facebook message, texte l me, emailed me, or called me, we would have spoken soon r. But, let's jump off LinkedIn, let's Facebook, text, emai , send a carrier pigeon, or a smoke signal, and you'll be able to get ahold of me quicker as we continue to com nunicate."

Being engaging, breaking the ice, and having a bit of hum r, is what started our back and forth banter. We emailed a co ple of times to move past the communication and into the c nversation. However, over a short while, it was then time to m ve into the collaboration, to create impact, income, and influ nce. Therefore, our next move was to meet in person— face o face. I decided to meet him where he was at—his office. Afte that meeting, it only took one week for me to be hired to do a resentation for his firm. This then led me to teaching his firm ny entire program, regarding how to be more effective com nunicators, while creating a NetWeb.

So, you see, the more you brush up on your communication skills, the more impact, income, and influence you receive. If you are constantly hiding behind your computer, these skills will begin to rust, and your results will prove it. As I said before, I too, create my NetWeb online; however, I am always sure to get face time with my new potential collaborators. I encourage you to do the same. Perhaps, getting out from behind your computer to meet people face to face, makes you nervous. I promise you, the more you practice the quicker you will perfect the skill. Understand, we all started somewhere; and if you remember correctly from my personal story, I made a ton of mistakes—I too had to start somewhere. So, no more excuses or complaints. Get out there and create your success!

CHAPTER 9
CARD COLLECTOR
VS
BUSINESS BUILDER

If I were to ask you to open your purse, open your desk drawer, clean out your glove compartment, or open your wallet, how many business cards would I find? How many of those business cards have been in there for one, two, or even three years? How many of those cards did you say you were going to follow up with, but never did? How many times, have you shuffled through those cards and thought, *I have a lot of leads.* How many times, have you said to yourself, *I'm going to call this one tomorrow?* How many times have you awaken at 7:30am to attend a meeting, just to collect cards?

When I'm in front of an audience speaking on this topic, I witness a room filled with people who are nodding their heads and laughing; because, they are all too familiar with being a card collector. Given the opportunity, I'll tell people, "I want to see in your purse or your bag. If I looked in your pockets right now, how many cards would I see?" The reality is, everyone has them; in fact, they have stacks of them.

Hey, don't be too hard on yourself if this is you.

However, stop doing this immediately. Collecting business cards, and shoving your card into the hands of others, is not doing business. Let's face it, you might as well stay home, and search the internet or the yellow pages to collect phone numbers. If you want to create a NetWeb, then you must stop being a card collector.

"Cami, I have a box of cards, stacks of them, they're everywhere. I have my file box filled with cards. I haven't called any of these people. What do I do with them?" Oddly enough, when we have a ton of business cards stored up, we have some security in thinking, "I have a lot of leads. I have all types of people who I can do business with." Truth is, you only have a lot of little pieces of paper with printing on them, and you're not doing anything with them. At this point, you might as well use them to wallpaper your bathroom.

In the next chapter, I will share with you the process of, what I call, cleaning up the wreckage of the past. This way, you can move forward powerfully, while no longer collecting cards; and instead, begin creating your NetWeb. Also, at the end of this book is, The Creed. The Creed, is all about committing to yourself that, you will no longer collect a single card; unless, you have full intentions of following-up with them, and you will do so within one week of obtaining their card. I encourage you to take a sneak peak in the back of the book and make this creed now.

The follow-up isn't about friending them on Facebook, following them on LinkedIn, sending out a bulk email, or sending an automated email. The follow-up is about reaching out, one-to-one; whether it be a written message or a phone call. If you are going to take the time to get acquainted with someone, and acquire their card, then you must commit to doing something with the card—other than shoving it in a drawer or a pocket. Now that you understand this, let's move on to learn, what you will do with all these cards that are a mirror of your mistake.

CHAPTER 10
CLEANING UP THE WRECKAGE

It's time! Yes, it's time to clean up the wreckage! It's time to get rid of all the cards, and follow-up with the leads. The cards are weighing you down. They are taking up space in your thoughts. You have a misconception that, these people are going to do business with you, just because their cards are in your desk. The only way they are, even possibly, going to do business with you, is if you, follow-up with them. So, this is exactly what I encourage you to do. Sit down, take a day (or however long it takes), and begin following-up.

Think about it—you have these people, who you promised to follow-up with, and you never did. Pointblank, you made a promise and didn't keep it. Perhaps, you didn't say the words "I promise" directly to them. However, asking for someone's contact information, speaks an unspoken promise to follow-up. Well, you didn't follow-up, so you broke your promise. Is this the reputation you want for yourself as a professional? If you want people to know, like, and trust you, so they will do business with you, then you must become a (wo)man of your word. You must show people that you are worthy of them knowing, liking, and trusting you. So, this means it's time to go back and keep your word. It's all about taking responsibility, by cleaning up your side of the street.

If you are sitting on cards that are months old, this requires a phone call—not a written message on some internet platform. Oh, I know…it's much easier to humble ourselves by hiding behind a computer screen. Well, tough. Your phone was created for a purpose—and a powerful purpose at that. Your phone is not just for texting…pick it up and use your voice.

Now, when you call these people, have your words prepared. Know your intended goal and use your words to get you there. For example, I would say something along the lines of, "Hey, Bob. Cami Baker here. I want to apologize. I met you three months ago, at a chamber event. I got your business card, and I meant to follow-up; but, unfortunately, I dropped the ball. I just want to apologize and open the communication. Do you have time for a quick conversation right now?" Guess what Bob always says? "Don't worry about it Cami, I should have called you too. How are you?" End of cleaning it up! Now just move on, build rapport, and talk about whatever you were going to talk about—invite him for coffee, offer a referral, and/or tell him about another networking event you heard about.

People are not sitting around thinking about you and why you haven't called—get over yourself. Address the big pink elephant you think is in the room and talk to them like you would any fiend. After all, that is what they would be if you treated them like one.

On another note, if you are calling someone who you really know, and who knows you well, your call would sound something like this: "Hey Bob, I know it's been a couple of years I thought about you on your birthday, and at Christmas. Shame on me that I haven't called." More times than not, their response sounds a bit like: "Hey, listen. Don't worry about it. I've been following you on Facebook. How are the kids?"

So, you see, making these phone calls are not scary. (FEAR—**F**alse **E**vidence **A**ppearing **R**eal.) Pick up the phone and begin the communication, so you can conversate to collaborate to get the impact, income, and influence you truly desire.

Let's talk about, what not to do. When making these phone calls, the worst thing you can do, is what most people do, which is, make excuses and mutter the words, *I'm sorry*. First of-all, there's a difference between saying, "I'm sorry" and "I apologize." It may mean the same thing to you; but, do you really want to put out to the universe that you are a sorry individual? Don't be sorry, instead apologize.

Saying, "I apologize" is how you own your mistakes, and sounds a bit like this: "Hey, listen. I made a promise to you. I said that I would send you an email with the link to another event. I dropped the ball. I apologize." Would you agree that, it sounds better than this: "Hey, listen, I got really busy and the kids were sick. The dog got hit by a car. The boss has been hard on me, and I never got back with you. Sorry."

You will find it to be very powerful, to simply, own it. Take responsibility and move forward. Consciously and subconsciously, people respect someone who can humble themselves by owning their mistakes, and then move forward. Nobody wants to hear your excuses. Nobody wants to hear how busy you've been. Guess what? We're all busy. Who cares? Nobody wants to hear that the kids were sick, or that your dog has fleas, or that the car wouldn't start. When it's somebody who knows you well, and you want to talk about the kids, the husband, and the boss, that's great; but, own your mistake before those conversations begin.

There was a point in my career, when I too, had to go back and call people from years ago—even from high school. It's just a matter of getting the fat elephant out of the room. Don't pretend the elephant doesn't exist. When you're calling someone who you haven't spoken with in years, don't pretend there's not any weird awkwardness; because, more than likely, there is (at least on your end, in your mind) Say, "I apologize" and move forward. This is how you clean up the wreckage. Once you clean up the wreckage, you can move forward powerfully as a productive, profitable, and professional networker, who creates a NetWeb. Be a player. Be a NetWebber. Strategize your way to success, by first, freeing yourself of all the contacts you have not contacted...that's why they call them contacts.

CHAPTER 11
NETWORKING IS A NOT
A PLACE WE GO

People tend to look at networking as a place that they go, or something that they put on their schedule. I used to feel the same way. I've said it many times, "I'm going to one of those networking things." I realized, networking is not a place that we go; rather, it is something that we do all the time. Anytime you communicate with someone (the minute you wake up and start sending messages online, the moment you call someone, introduce yourself at a sporting event, Starbucks, or anywhere of the liking), you are networking.

Several months ago, I had on my calendar to attend an event at the Hard Rock Café in Boston, MA. Yes, it was one of those *networking things...ugh.* Yes, even me, who has attended, spoken at, and hosted thousands upon thousands of events, felt that way. It was in the moment of those thoughts, that a light bulb went on inside my head, *Cami, if this is what you, and everyone else does, every day every time we communicate, then why must it feel so dreary? Why look at it as, something I must go to? Why not make it fun? Why not begin to view it as an opportunity to meet new people— to mingle? Why not view it as an opportunity to create resources, relationships, and revenue that rocks?*

When you view networking as a "must do" and a "drag", then your emotions are going to feel it. When you begin to see networking as creating a NetWeb, and as an opportunity to build your empire by communicating and conversating, you will begin to see the results you dream of. What it boils down to is your mindset. You have set your mind to believe networking is work. I encourage you to reset your mind by viewing networking as NetWebbing—Networking wastes time with mindless activity, while NetWebbing leverages time through planned strategy. All-in-all, it becomes "play" to do something, when you know you will achieve an end goal—as opposed to abstractly showing up.

We will be getting into more about your mindset in the next chapter. For now, begin with the basics. Begin telling yourself, "I'm going out to play." When someone ask you, "What are you doing tonight?" Tell them, "I'm going out to play." When you respond with "I'm going out to play", you will love the responses you then receive in return. They will sound a bit like this: "What do you mean, you're going out to play?" "Where are you going to go play at?" "How are you playing?" "Can I come along, too?" Can you imagine how the tables will flip? Where you once begged people to come along to an event with you, they now begin to ask you if they can come with you. Trust me, it really does happen this way! It's all about your mindset, and how you relay your mindset to others through your words and actions.

Responding that way, changed how I was being perceived and received in the marketplace. All I did was simply fix my own mindset, and others followed suit. Switch your thoughts from: *What leads am I going to get tonight? Will I get a contract signed? How many business cards can I collect?* To: *Who can I play with tonight? Who is going to play with me in my sandbox tonight? Who am I going to get to meet?*

That particular evening, at the Hard Rock Café, I showed up on fire. I was excited to be there! Yes, even for me, that is impressive; because, look, I'm a human being, too. Sometimes, I too, would rather be at home with a good book and curled up on the couch. But, because I showed up on fire, the results were just as hot. I had many doors open for me that night and I met people I never would have met, had I gone there with the attitude of dread. Just know, whatever results you produce are a result of your attitude, and failure to apply what you know. So, if you are ready to have doors open for you, all the while having a blast, simply, change your mindset. Now are you ready to go play in the sandbox?

PART 3
CREATING A NETWEBB

CHAPTER 12
MINDSET VS. SKILLSET

Now that I have addressed all the comments, questions, and misconceptions about networking, it's time I teach you, in depth, the *how to*. Too often, we read books, and hear great teachings; yet, we never get the full, *how to,* when it comes to applying what we have just learned. How do we start a great conversation? How do we make a great first impression? How do we feel comfortable in our own skin? How do we get business to come to us? How do we grow large enough to impact the world? How do we up our game as a minge to millions maverick?

I have been the shark saying, "Dun-dun-dun-dun-dun-dun." I have also been the prey, screaming in my head, "Oh no", while running from someone who were aggressively chasing me. Now I'm in the beautiful place where, I now, have the blessing and the honor, of being someone who can stand still while rising quickly—I have people who come to me to do business. That's what I want to teach you—my tribe. When we stop repelling, we begin attracting. Let's stop sharking—chasing people. Let's intentionally start attracting the resources, relationships, and revenue that rock.

Your first step towards becoming a powerful, professional, productive, profitable NetWebber, is understanding mindset vs. skillset. Although a hot mess in my early days (when it came to networking), I did at least, understand the power of reading and mentors. My first mentor, back when I was in real estate, gave me a book by Price Pritchett, titled *You Squared*. It was a booklet, with a little less than forty pages—perfect for my two-hour flight.

This book taught about, how people take tiny steps and incremental changes, when instead, they should be leaping. When you make the leap, you find your wings on your way down. This concept helped me to realize, *I don't have to make teeny-tiny baby steps. I can just leap into the next way of being.* That one little booklet, launched me into development and growth— both personal and professional, and emotional and spiritual. When you realize the power of one book, you will realize the power of many books. This is exactly why I encourage you to, if you're not already, begin reading regularly. In the back of this book you will find, a list of the books I highly recommend you read. These are books that will not only launch you; but will propel you into the success you have always dreamt of.

I don't know if you remember cassettes; but, back in the day, I had a cassette player in my car. In this cassette player, you would find, the audio of *Feel the Fear and Do It Anyway* by Susan Jeffers. I listened to that cassette over and over, again. The more I listened and educated myself, the hungrier I became—I kept on learning more, and more. Over time, I studied self-development techniques, neuro-linguistic programming, body language, mirroring, matching, and more. I also studied under Tony Robbins, Zig Ziglar, and other successful influencers.

I teach, and stand by, that every person (whether a mentor to others or not), should have a mentor. No matter what level you are at, there is always someone who knows more, who can teach you more, and who can help you rise to your next level. It is important that you work on your mindset, before your skill set. Many people, think because they studied a trade, they have the skill, and with the skill they will be successful. How wrong this thinking is. You can have all the skill in the world, but if your mindset sucks, your personal life and business life, will indeed, suck.

At the time of this book being written, it was sixteen years ago, when my mindset began to drastically change. I was a real estate agent, who was just beginning to climb out of a hole, that I dug myself into. My mind was not as clear as it is today; and I was a single mother overcoming addictions and low self-esteem. At the agency I was working at, I began to reach a point where I had to get out into the world and meet people—network. Joan (my angel), is a lady who had been a real estate agent for about thirty years; and she was watching me. She could tell I was hungry and tenacious; and dare I say, desperate. I was in survival mode, shark mode, and was on the hunt. Needless-to-say, I wasn't presenting myself in a favorable manner. Joan, of course noticed, and came to me saying, "Cari, I have a suit that I have outgrown. I would love to give it to you. Would you like to have it?" Not only did I need a suit, but this was Joan's suit. She was someone who everyone highly respected. She was very demure; yet, a very powerful business woman. She was a center of influence, and a true example for me.

When she offered me this suit, I graciously said "Yes, I'd love to have it!" She brought it in from her car, and I was in awe. It was the power color of red, and consisted of a blazer, a skirt, and even, red shoes. To add to my excitement, it fit me perfectly. All that was left for me to do was, purchase a blouse to go underneath it. When I walked out in the suit to show Joan, she said, "You look like a million bucks! How about it, kid?"

For quite some time, I wore that suit to every appointment. Needless-to-say, I was a bit worried that I only had one suit, and I felt as though it was the only attire everyone always saw me in. However, Joan eased my mind by teaching me, "Don't worry about changing your suit, just change your audience." What she meant was, make sure that you're reaching out to new people every day.

There seemed to be magic in this suit. When I wore it on appointments, I felt powerful, I held my shoulders back further than usual, and my head higher than ever. However, after presenting myself in the red suit to a new contact, I would begin establishing a more down-to-earth relationship by saying, "Now that you have met me in my red suit and we like each other, I just want you to know, next time, I will be wearing my jeans." This always made them laugh and agreed to the more relaxed atmosphere next time.

It's amazing how, one red suit can change a life. From the perspective that one woman (Joan), cared enough about me to the way wearing it made me feel powerful, my life began to transform. Coming from being a single mom, who was accustomed to earning $500 a week, to a top 5% earning agent in our company, earning $5,000 from each commission check a couple times a month, Cami Baker, became a woman to be reckoned with.

About six months into my soaring, Joan (with a grin on her face), took me to the side, and said, "Cami, you know that suit that I gave you a few months ago?" I said, "Yes, Joan. I absolutely do. I love that suit. I wear it all the time. Thank you so much!"

She said, "Well, I have a little confession to make."

"Okay, what is it?"

"I didn't outgrow that suit. I could see that you needed one, so I bought it for you."

"Joan, that's so nice of you! Umm, that was so gracious of you to do that."

"Well, not only did I buy it for you, but, I bought it from the Salvation Army."

We giggled and laughed about it. Then we hugged, and I said, "You know what? I'm so glad that you did. This suit has made all the difference in the world to me." Then, she added, "Not only did I buy it for you from the Salvation Army, it was on sale, on the $3 rack."

Joan was brilliant enough, not only to see that I needed a boost in my appearance, but to tell me a little white lie, so I wasn't embarrassed or humiliated by her offer. She was also, brilliant with her timing, to come to me a few months later because, she wanted to be honest. I believe, she knew that I could see the lesson— it's not what we wear, rather it's how we wear it. You see, I wouldn't have acquired the skills as an agent, nor the skills of a netwebber, if I hadn't put that suit on and felt powerful.

It was about three years into being an agent, when I hired my own assistant, Monique. Monique was the type of person who was good at her job; but, had her days of coming in with the, *woe-is-me* attitude. "I don't have enough money. My kids don't have what they need for Christmas." Now, mind you, she was smoking cigarettes at about $7 a pack, and stopping to get a Big Gulp every day. So, one day over coffee, I shared the story of the red suit with her. Then I said, "You know what, Monique? I'm going to get you licensed as an agent, and as I have buyers coming to the table for my listings, I'm going to give you some buyers."

I wanted to help her out. I wanted to give her the leg up that Joan had given me. However, once she got her license, the excuses continued. "Well Cami, I don't have a nice enough car to drive people in. I don't have gas money to put in the car, to take people on appointments. I don't have the right clothes to wear."

Monique had chosen the mindset, that most others do too, *Have-Do-Be*. "I must have, so that I can do, so that I can be." I must have the right clothes, before I can go to the right networking event. I must have the right amount of money in my pocket, before I can pay to go to a $20 event. I must have enough time, before I can go work out, so I can be healthy."

I encourage you to take a moment and self-reflect. Is this your same mentality? Are you waiting to have, before you do, so that you can be? If so, this is your number one problem, that is standing in the way of your success. Think about it. Think back to Red (the pet name I call my powerful red suit). Just as I explained to Monique, I will explain to you. The suit cost Joan $3. It could have cost me $3. To be more matter-of-fact, it didn't cost Joan or me anything; rather it was an investment. A $3 investment, that would change the course of my level of success.

Through all the complaints and excuses you find yourself making, are you saying that you can't invest a few bucks at the Salvation Army, or to attend an event? If a red suit, changes your attitude like it had mine, then I assure you, you need to go today and invest. Go a day without your Big Gulp, your Starbucks coffee, or your Twinkie, and make a purchase that will change the course of your career. The overall question for you to consider is: What is your success worth to you? What are you willing to sacrifice now, for the sake of your future? I guarantee you, if it must be a $100 suit, it will be worth the investment.

Find what it is, that brings out the powerhouse that resides within you. That red suit changed my mindset from, *woe-is-me* to *I can do this! I am powerful! I love my part! I am being the part!* It set me on a path to when someone asked me, "Cami can you do this? Can you do that?" My answer was always, "Yes I can!" What is it for you, that will push you into the right mindset? Perhaps, it's not a red suit. Whatever it is though, it's time for you to invest. Find one small, inexpensive investment that will transform your mindset from: *I must HAVE "x", in order to DO "Y" so that I'll BE "Z"* to *I will BE that which I want, so that I DO what that person would do, and therefore I will HAVE what that person would have!*

I encourage you to invest in your mind. Read some books, find a mentor, and watch and listen to educational programs. Turn off your country music, rap, or heavy metal, and instead, listen to audio books. Listen to content that will change the course of your career. When you are truly ready to communicate to conversate to collaborate, to create impact, income, and influence, so you build resources, relationships, and revenue that rocks, then stand up tall, put your shoulders back, hold your head high, invest in your success and your mind.

CHAPTER 13
BLUE MARLINS ARE NOT FOUND IN FISHBOWLS

When we talk about really upping our game as a networker, there are decisions you need to make. First, decide if you truly want to begin communicating to conversate to collaborate, to create impact, income, and influence. Then decide if you want to do so on a local, regional, national, or global level. Once you make those decisions, you can now begin laying out your personalized roadmap to success. No matter which level you desire, there are certain steps that you must take. For example, say you desire to remain at a local level, you must travel global to grow local. Why? Simply put, knowledge is power. Sure, it may be outside of your comfort zone to travel, to rub elbows with millionaires, and to even associate with other cultures. If this is true to you, well, too bad...suck it up buttercup. You do want to impact lives with your business, right? You do want to earn more income, right? Well, then, you must travel global.

When you travel outside of your normalcy, your mind begins to expand. You learn new techniques, grow in your confidence, and bring back to your community new knowledge and resources. All-in-all, you become more valuable in your industry, and in your community. The more value you offer, the more impact you have, and the more income you earn.

Blue Marlins are among the largest, fastest, and most recognizable fish in the world. These fish stand out amongst all the other fish in the ocean. A female blue marlin can get as large as fourteen feet in length and weigh more than 1,985 pounds. Bottomline, Blue Marlins are not found in fish bowls.

Your network is either a fish bowl or an ocean. Most people reside in the fishbowl. They network with cute little goldfish, with big dreams and big hearts; yet, small amounts of determination and dedication—or perhaps, misguided determination and dedication.

I want you to look around you. Are you networking in a fishbowl? Are your conversations resembling ground hog's day? Are your days on repeat? Same people, same action, same results, and same amount of comfort? Are the cute little goldfish you swim with holding you back? Do you desire to be a Blue Marlin, and swim with other Blue Marlins? Well, you cannot attract other Blue Marlins if you stay in the fishbowl.

I assure you, if you have been in a fishbowl most of your life, when you decide to swim with the Blue Marlins, you will be uncomfortable. But, rest assured, success does not lie in the arms of comfort; rather it lies in the arms of discomfort. Most people would teach you to, *get out of your comfort zone*. I won't do that. Instead, I encourage you to expand your comfort zone. When you are always comfortable, you will not grow. When you don't grow, you don't change. When you don't change, you produce the same old redundant results.

I have been a networker, for about sixteen years. I have

been an entrepreneur since, I was eight. I have forty, plus, years of an entrepreneurial mindset, and thirty years of being on stages. Despite my journey and experience, daily, I am still faced with situations that make me uncomfortable. Every day, I must decide to allow myself to be uncomfortable. When you can see what awaits you on the other side of the discomfort, you will find it is worth the moments of being uncomfortable.

What tends to happen to people is, they can't see past the discomfort. They sense discomfort and they turn around. The next time you find yourself faced with a decision, to allow yourself to be uncomfortable or turn around, I want you to stop and look past the discomfort—what awaits you on the other side. Ask yourself, *If I allow myself to be uncomfortable for twenty minutes, an hour, a day, a week, a month, or even a year, what results will come of it?* Once you have the vision of the glorious results, perhaps, you will decide to step into your inner Blue Marlin and come create your NetWeb as you play your way to success, doing the very thing that scares you.

Do you find yourself going to events that are free and/or convenient? When was the last time you began to build a relationship with someone who is faster, stronger, and wiser than you? You know, someone who makes you feel inadequate, because of your own inner desire to live up to them.

First, let me assure you, successful people love to teach, mentor, and help others reach their next level. This means, there is no reason for you to feel inadequate. Second, if you naturally feel that way in someone's presence, then that is exactly who you should be swimming with. It means that person is a Blue Marlin. It's like mama always said, "You become who you hang around." If you want to remain a little cute goldfish in your tiny fish bowl, then by all means, remain in the fishbowl. But, since you are reading this book, it is my educated guess that, you desire more than anything, to be a Blue Marlin. So, ask yourself: *Who do I need to be associating with? Who out there is faster, stronger, and wiser than me? Whose behaviors will I rob and duplicate? Whose shoes will I step into?*

Now, I'm not saying that you can't make great contacts in the fishbowl, because you can, and I have. About a year ago, I was at a free local meetup event. Although, I encourage you to get out of the fish bowl, you should still be stopping by the fish bowl for a visit, when you have the extra time. Notice I say, *extra time.* In other words, fish bowls always come second to Blue Marlin events.

At this free local meet-up I attended, there were about forty people in attendance. I'm meeting people, shaking hands, kissing babies, and striking up conversations. All-in-all, I was positioning myself to be memorable. I made sure I stood out, by applying everything I am teaching you in this book. As I am going about being the Blue Marlin in the fishbowl, I found myself standing in a group, talking to each other about the importance of not asking: *What do you do?* Well, wouldn't you know, a guy walks up, interrupts, and ask us, "What do you all do?" Of course, we all began laughing, and of course, I began to banter with him by saying, "Well, what we are doing right here, right now, is talking about not asking people *what do you do?*

Needless-to-say, Ron Couming and I hit it off, exchanged business cards, followed-up on Facebook, and began conversating and collaborating. Overtime, I found myself on the phone with him, listening to him invite me to an event in Chicago. This event consisted of internet marketing experts and multimillionaires, who can launch me to my next level, by putting me on global stages. The next thing I knew I was on a plane from Boston to Chicago.

At the event in Chicago, I am introduced to a gentleman named, Bill Walsh. Bill runs the Rainmaker organization, and host events all over the world. From here, I begin attending events all over the world, and continue to see Bill at the same events. Overtime, the two of us built a business relationship, that resulted in him inviting me to a networking event, hosted at his mansion. At this event, there were Blue Marlins swimming everywhere.

While there, I headed over to a table of Blue Marlins, and introduced myself to a gentleman named, Erik Swanson. Erik Swanson host conferences three times a year in the United States and globally, called: *Habitude Warrior*. Of course, the two of us hit it off, began building a business relationship, and speaking on stages at events—my network expanded, and so did my impact, income, and influence.

Now remember, I first met Ron in a fishbowl, and then I said "Yes" to swimming in the ocean (Chicago), and from there I began swimming with Blue Marlins. The overall point I want you to see and learn is, when you have extra time, swim in the fishbowl, say "Yes" to the ocean, and swim with the Blue Marlins. When you understand this system, you will grow to know, like, and trust it. Once you know, like, and trust it, the system will prove itself to you—it works.

Furthermore, it is important to be careful in the fishbowl. The fishbowl is comfortable, and when comfort sneaks up on us, and when we're not careful, we tend to get too comfortable and stay longer than we should. If you find yourself in a fishbowl for too long, with the same complacent fish, walk away. Your goal is to create a NetWeb with those who are also only, visiting the fish bowl—just like the guy I met, who invited me to Chicago. You see, that day I visited the fish bowl, he did too. He is accustomed to swimming with Blue Marlins, but when he has time, he remembers that there is usually a Blue Marlin visiting the fishbowl. Learn to recognize a Blue Marlin in a fishbowl, connect with them, and then get out.

Of course, the story doesn't end with Erik, who hosts the *Habitude Warrior Conference*. You see, once you meet one Blue Marlin, you just keep on meeting more, and more of them. So, I'm speaking at one of the *Habitude Warrior Conferences*, and there was a woman there by the name of Jennifer Lier. Jennifer's position is to book keynote speakers— exactly who I need to know. Of course, the old Cami, wanted to transform from a Blue Marlin to a shark. However, fortunately, I controlled myself, and remained a Blue Marlin.

So, it was my turn to speak. I hit the stage, was on top of my game, the audience loved me, and the impact I desired to produce was produced. As I exited the stage, I ventured into the green room, where I could take a deep breath of success. When I was finished with my break, I stepped out into the foyer, and to my surprise, I was approached by a woman with a business card. As she handed me her card, she says, "My name is Jennifer Lier. I book keynote speakers, and I look for three things: content, material that is good, and a confident stage presence. You have them in spades, and I would like to represent you."

Now, if you remember correctly, my sharking mindset was going to go find this woman. Thank God I followed my intuition and practiced what I preach. I didn't have to find her, she found me. To think, this all began with one gentleman in a fishbowl, and my wisdom to know not to stay in the fishbowl.

So, I encourage you to consider who it is you swim with. Is it in a fishbowl, or the ocean? Are you comfortable or uncomfortable? Can you now begin to see what awaits you on the other side of the uncomfortable? If you do, then I am sure I will be seeing you in the ocean at one time or another.

CHAPTER 14
MAKE MONEY
WHILE MAKING A DIFFERENCE

What the heck is *Cause Marketing*? Imagine if you could take the one thing you are most passionate about supporting, and incorporate your fundraising, awareness raising, and volunteering efforts while making money.

The planet is in a wonderful phase of transition. Those of us who are visionaries, heart centered, forward thinkers, and called to be a contribution to the world are coming forth in a powerful way. Because of this, there are many causes that are getting the attention they deserve, and impact is being felt in a beautiful way.

Cause refers to any cause, mission, organization, group of people, group of animals, community awareness, or situation that the Entrepreneur or Business is inspired to support, contribute to, or otherwise be affiliated with, in an effort to give back and pay it forward.

Marketing in this context means strategically using the efforts and engagement with the cause in such a way that the Entrepreneur or Business is able to market themselves because of it. Showing their marketplace that they are leaders, givers, stewards of giving, and not just concerned about the planet, but taking action to do something about it.

Cause Marketing is partnering, pairing, and positioning your passion and purpose with your business' success!

Many people want to do more, yet are waiting until they have the time, money, or influence to do it. Or, they are doing wonderful works in the world, yet allowing it to take time away from their business and costing them even more money. There is a misconception for some that they should keep their good deeds anonymous, send a check in a quiet manner, and not toot their own horn about volunteering.

Cause Marketing gives you a way to let anyone and everyone know you are proud to be a contribution, and you encourage others to also contribute. It gives you something to promote other than your business, and in doing so, it gives you the ability to build rapport and have the marketplace get to know, like, and trust you. As we all know, people do business with people they know, like, and trust. Therefore, Cause Marketing is a win-win for everyone. The cause gets more funding, more volunteers, more awareness, and grows because of the activities that take place. Your business has a platform to be seen, received, and perceived as actively giving to society and the planet. Those who are enrolled to participate in the activities with you, always get more from being a part of the event than then what they gave.

One mainstream version of Cause Marketing that you may recognize is Starkist Tuna. In the 1990's, Starkist started promoting that their tuna was "Dolphin Safe." They made a business decision to only use tuna that was captured without harming dolphins in the process. They could have done this from a moral position and not told anyone; however, they were smart enough to let the whole world know they backed a cause. They let their marketplace know that when they bought Starkist tuna, they were backing a company that cared about the animals. The consumer was, and still is, willing to pay more for the brand that cares than the ones who don't.

In a very competitive market, savvy businesses know that when push comes to shove, when all things are equal, when it is a toss-up as to which brand or professional to give the credit card to, the customer takes into consideration who makes them feel good about their spending decisions. Starkist can charge more per can of tuna, simply because it makes others feel good to support a business because of what they stand for. The same goes for your business. Your business will also win the toss-up when the differentiating factor is that it feels good to support you and your business over the competition, all because of what you stand for and believe in.

They want to give me money? I first learned about Cause Marketing by total accident. I was doing it for years before I even realized I was doing it. The short version of this story is:

As a real estate agent, I was a networking fool. I was on the hunt, in the trenches, beating the bushes...you pick the analogy. I had a vision board on my wall with a Mustang convertible; but, not just any Mustang convertible, it was a 1964 ½, vintage—like Thelma and Louise over the cliff. The kind everyone knows is cool.

One of my commission checks on a large building made my dream a reality, and Scoop (the name given to my Mustang), was acquired. She received her name because of the scoop in the hood (which flew off while I was going down the highway the first weekend I had her; but, I'll save that story for another time).

Scoop was white with black interior, and the top was black (although, I never drove her with the top up). I had an assistant at the time who was calling around finding parades and car shows to put Scoop in. I had CamiBaker.com magnets all over her and loved using her to market myself because she turned every eye.

One of the places we called was a local Old Home Day annual event. All the small towns had one, and lots of them had car shows. This one said "No, we don't have an antique car show, but we would love to have one. Would you like to sponsor it?" I said, "Yes! Yes, I would!" From there, the fun began!

The first year we hosted the antique car show, I paid for everything and was not intending on making money from the show itself; rather, from the marketing opportunity

it gave me. As people started arriving in their cars, they were all coming to register with cash in hand. I was so naive and green, I didn't know enough about antique car shows to know they actually pay to get in them. (Great learning point here. Fake it until you make it. Don't wait until you figure something out to do it. Set it into motion and you will figure it out as you go.)

So, my assistant Monique says, "If they are going to hand us money we should take it!" We didn't that year, but the next year I thought more about it and decided that I didn't personally want to make money off the car show, but that I could donate to a cause just to be nice. After asking around, I found *Live and Let Live Farm* who rescues horses. They were a great partner because, many people in the area knew them, respected them, supported them, and volunteered with them. I didn't know it when I choose to give them a couple thousand dollars a year from the car show, but it all came into play.

As the next year's show was coming around I had flyers made that reflected the event and the Live and Let Live Farm. All-of-a-sudden,  the conversations while promoting the event were much different. It wasn't Cami Baker the realtor doing a car show; instead, it was an antique car show put on for the betterment and contribution to this wonderful organization (the cause), that as it turned out, everyone already knew and loved!

I could walk into as many businesses as I wanted to and NetWeb with business people. The scene was just me and a flyer. No business cards, briefcase, or sales pitch. Just me saying "I'm helping in sponsoring an antique car show, where the proceeds go to the Live and Let Live Farm. I was hoping you could help us by letting me hang this in your window and spread the word." In doing this, here is what happened:

Out of every ten flyers I passed out, on average:

- 3 would be disengaged.
- 3 would say, "Sure leave it there, and we'll put it up."
- 3-4 would say things like: "I love antique cars!" or "I know that farm, our church volunteers there!" or a combination of something positive, engaging, and friendly. This built instant rapport, bridged the humanity gap, and gave me a way to meet people and create the resources, relationships, and revenue that I wanted; all the while, helping a worthy cause with fundraising, community awareness raising, and media coverage.

This can work similarly for social media and online marketing; however, at the time, I was doing business locally and only in real estate. Meeting people face-to-face was, and still is, the best way to build the *know, like, and trust* factor.

Besides the flyers I handed out, I could also email blast or call (yes call, the phone dials out too), my past, present, and future clients to let them know about the car show. Asking if they would like to come enjoy the day with us, bring a car to the show, refer those they know with cars, and get a booth to promote their business at the show. I cannot count how many deals I made with people who I reached out to about the car show where the conversation turned to, "So how's the market?"

Moreover, I invited the media to come and cover the events, in which they did. The Live and Let Live Farm would come to the events with their banners and their favorite little Mule on a leash for the kids to pet. It was beautiful! They received exposure, CamiBaker.com received exposure, the farm received money, the cars had a great time, and so it went for seven years just like that.

Then I mixed it up by bringing Big Max (the RE/MAX hot air balloon), to the events along with the Boys and Girls clubs. I did an event at Hampton Beach called "Life's a Beach", where (because of the event and the cause), I was able to get a dozen loan companies, title companies, and home inspectors to donate beach toys, lunch, and t-shirts with all our logos! We had Big  Max at the Boys and Girls clubs giving tethered rides while we did face painting, karate demos, and grilled hamburgers and hot dogs. Big Max and RE/MAX had a *Challenge the Winds* campaign where RE/MAX would educate the school about hot air ballooning and then come out early in the mornings and roll the huge and impressive balloon out on the field to inflate and give tethered rides to the teachers and any public figures who showed up. This took place at a local school with me, Monique, Scoop, 1500 students, the Mayor, the Media, and lots of free publicity for CamiBaker.com.

During those ten years I was ignorance on fire! I was getting as many people to events as possible to raise the most money, the most awareness, and get the most media coverage for all involved and my business. However, I was learning during the process how to *Make Money while Making a Difference*.

Here are some reasons why it is smart to participate in Cause Marketing:

- A way to network without the boring networking meetings.
- Create your own networks and networking situations.
- If at a boring networking meeting you can stand out, be different, and be memorable.
- The cause you partner with, becomes part of your network to do business with.
- You are seen and received by your partners as someone being a contribution and you will create resources, relationships, and revenue in most cases.
- It gives you a reason to contact the media. (No one cared about a real estate agent doing a car show. They cared about a wonderful cause being helped. They would show up with camera in hand.)
- Gives you reason to reach out to past clients, current

clients, and potential future clients by letting them know the fundraiser or event is happening.

- It opens the door for conversations, keeps you top of mind, and gives you an opportunity to touch customers that can lead to immediate business.
- Helps get more volunteers, board members, and funds for the cause.
- Recruit more teammates/sales associates.
- Build rapport with those at the event.
- Sales people want to be associated with businesses who are visionaries, contributions to society, and who have stuff going on, so they too can have fun while making money and a difference.
- People want to do business with businesses who make a difference. If all things are equal, and you are doing cause marketing and your competition is not, guess who wins the customer?

Case Study: Success in Cause Marketing

My client Jon Morton is the perfect example of how this works. Jon wanted to build his Network Marketing business and came to me for strategy around how to meet people in a new way. He had watched me have success in Network Marketing and in Real Estate. After a couple of years seeing me on Social Media, he observed how I took a stand for what I was passionate about, and how I transitioned from those businesses into being an Author and Speaker by simply declaring it to be. I used the method I talk about in this book of *Be, Do, Have,* and stepped into *Being* an Author and Speaker.

Once you take on the *Being* part, you then are in a position of *Doing* what you want to do. Naturally, you will then

Have what you want to have. This caught his attention, and after a qualifying conversation, the relationship of consulting Jon as his Business Coach began.

I first asked Jon what he was passionate about. I explained to him that if he were to network and build relationships with people in a whole new way, so people would receive and perceive him, he needed to know in what way he wanted to be received and perceived. He told me he was very passionate about veterans, because he himself is one. He also said that animals touch his heart as he has rescue dogs. This is a perfect combination of passions.

In Cause Marketing you are wanting to attract people to you and create common ground to build rapport on. It is best to focus on groups and causes that are universal—in that, most can agree on the urgency of helping. For example, the elderly, children, veterans, animals, and environment; to include the issues they face like hunger, cancer, or abuse. I encourage you to avoid politics, religion, or sports, because no matter which side you are on there will be those who are opposed. Remember, you are looking to create meaningful, masterful conversations and rapport, not open yourself up to criticism or defending your position.

As a side note, if your passion truly is of a religious, political, or sport nature, might I suggest that you still do your Cause Marketing around something less controversial. You will still be making a difference while you make money, and when your business is making more money because of your Cause Marketing, you will ultimately have the resources, relationships, and revenue to build a new church, spread the Word, or anything else you want to do with the funds.

Taking you back to Jon, animals and veterans was a double scoop of yumminess! His first assignment was to decide if he wanted to create his own movement or jump on the bandwagon someone else had already created. Let's look at the pros and cons of this part of the equation.

To create your own movement takes much more effort, and you are starting from ground zero. Therefore, there is no community to tap into (which I will discuss more when we talk about existing organizations).

Creating your own movement has these elements:

- It's your baby! (Which can be good or bad.)
- You make all the rules and decisions. (Once again, can be good or bad.)
- You can bring awareness to something, that perhaps, is not already being addressed and supported.
- As a Maverick, independent thinker, lone wolf kind of personality, you don't have to answer to others or ask for permission.
- You don't know if it will work because it's not proven.
- If you want it to be an official nonprofit, you have a lot of paperwork and expenses.
- If a board is to be created, you must take the time to pull those people together…there are a lot of variables that will make or break doing your own thing.

Here are the pros to partnering with an already existing group of people:

- Ease of stepping in and simply raising your hand to participate.
- They already have established themselves and have a

platform.

- There is an immediate network of people to network with.
- They will already have activities, events, fundraisers...ect, that you can get involved with.
- If they don't have pre-existing activities, you can offer to create one, and there will already be structure in place to help with your event.
- They could have an email list in the thousands, a large following of supporters, monthly meetings...etc, that are available for you to put to good use in helping to promote what you are doing. For example, if you want to hold a fundraising event in their honor, they could email blast their list of 10,000 about it, knowing that the more successful your event is the better it is for them.
- If the group has been around a long time (for example, The Ronald McDonald House or American Cancer Society), you will have instant name recognition and credibility for being associated with them.

To decide to jump on someone else's bandwagon, you will first want to decide if your focus is:

- Local
- Regional
- National
- International

Jon wanted to meet people locally; so, he needed to find an organization that even if they were on a global scale, they would have a local branch that he could tap into and support. For him, finding an already established group was more to his liking, and so he set out to find just the right one.

After much research, a few emails, and phone calls, Jon landed on an organization called, Hero Pups. This well deserving, pre-existing group was only about a year old when Jon met the founder Laura Barker. He was moved by their mission of assisting not only Veterans, but also first responders in partnering them with a Pup Companion. Pup Companions, gives both the Hero and their pup the love and support each needs to lead happy, joyful lives.

I taught Jon about how to position, posture, package, and present himself to Hero Pups in such a way that they would see his passion and desire to, not just be a typical volunteer, but to be a leader and major contribution to their cause. With just the right wording, body language, and good old fashion sincerity, Jon was as thick as thieves with Laura, and a beautiful partnership of contribution to the betterment of all was created!

As the months progressed, Jon was not just added to the board, he was made the Media Representative for HeroPups.com, and has now stepped into the leadership position of doing interviews on behalf of the organization. Radio, Social Media, print, videos, and all forms of spreading the word about their mission is now his mission. This gives him a whole new way of networking, meeting others, and building rapport.

Instead of going to the typical boring networking meeting and giving the played out 30-second elevator pitch that everyone else does, Jon uses that time to talk about Hero Pups, and often receives a standing ovation after his Dirty-30. Even more, he receives invites to speak about the organization. Imagine, if you will, a professional and well-groomed business man who shows up with a cute puppy under one arm and a U.S. Veteran by his side, all sharing the heartwarming story of how putting two heroes together has saved and transformed the lives of many. There is never a dry eye in the place!

Now what does all this have to do with building business and making money? Well, first impressions are everything. People are not meeting Jon as he is pitching a product, begging for referrals, or telling them how great he and his service is. They are meeting an entrepreneur who is a philanthropist and is being a contribution to something much

120

bigger than himself.

Moreover, the audience has the opportunity to talk about how their father is also a veteran, they too have rescue dogs, sure they would love to sponsor this next event, or how they can get involved and feel good about it. Now when the conversation turns to "What do you do?", or business of any sort, these people have been given the blessing of having met Jon on mutually respectful ground and they know, like, and trust him before it ever came up. This gives him an advantage. Not to take advantage, but to have the advantage of having learned how to NetWeb through the *Mingled to Millions* planned strategy.

A couple of ancillaries that have come out of it are the increase in Jon's position at his career due to his ability to position himself with such confidence that his boss recognized it. Also, he now sees himself in a new light and is now writing a book titled, *Who Rescued Who*. Their presence in his life has given him such meaning, and now through this series of events, a much larger platform to be a contribution than he ever would have dreamed has come his way.

Are you passionate about children's right? Preventing animal abuse? Bringing awareness to human trafficking? Giving love to Alzheimer patients because someone was there for your grandparent when they needed it? Feeding the homeless? Helping single mothers, or assisting people who are down on their luck get back on their feet? All these missions and so many more have been touched through my clients and Cause Marketing. All my clients who wanted to partner their passion with their pocketbook were able to do so with the *Mingle to Millions* planned strategy.

The best way to help someone who needs help, is to have resources, relationships, and revenue at your fingertips, so that you can help in a big way. Anything worth doing is worth letting the world know you are doing it and asking if they too want to be a contribution!

Jon has said to me, "I feel so good knowing my actions are making a difference that I want others to know how good it can make them feel too! I started this journey with you Cami to network differently and build my business. I was not expecting to have this kind of joy added to my life. It is now my mission, to not only support Hero Pups and what we stand for, but also to inspire others to be a contribution to whatever cause turns them on and have this same fulfillment in their lives that I feel every day! Thank you!"

Cause Marketing with the Ronald McDonald House

Lowell Cares Car Show with
Hope Dove Inc and Cami Baker
getting a letter of recognition
from the Mayer of Lowell

PART 4
INTERVIEWS

CONVERSATION WITH RON SUKENICK

Cami Baker:

"Hi my networking friends! Cami Baker here, from CamiBaker.com. I am here with one of my newer networking buddies, Ron Sukenick."

Ron Sukenick:

"What a treat to be speaking with you today, Cami! I can't believe it took this long!"

Cami Baker:

"I think we met, maybe less than a month ago, and this is the beauty for those who are reading our interview here today. It's the beauty of being able to communicate and conversate, because when you can communicate with someone and have a nice conversation, the collaboration just flows. As my system flows…now we're in the collaboration mode; and I just love that! The reason why we're on this call, is because about a month ago, through a series of quirky events, Ron and I were introduced (because we're both networking experts), and now here we are. I am just blown away by the success that Ron has had, the books that he's written, the years and years that he has on me of experience in networking. I am humbled, and I am a student today, and I want to learn from you, Ron: How you got started in networking? What it has done for you personally and in your business life? And, some tips for everyone. Just let us hear it. Give us all your yummy goodness."

Ron Sukenick:

"Thank you Cami. Look, I love people. In between all the

conversations any of us can ever have, there are always people, and people always do business with people they meet, they feel comfortable with, they like, and they trust. It all began with just loving people. I'm not sure how that happened, but I can share this with everybody. All the success I've ever had, four books published, national speaker for the Office of the Secretary of Defense, training department...All kinds of stuff. I've never ever, Cami, ever had any success without the help of people."

"When did it all start? For me, it started in the mid '70's. Think about that for a second. No email, obviously no websites...just people. It was all face-to-face. I was in the real estate business and doing great; but, it was really my ability to get out and talk, and it was my ability to know those eight magic words. I always needed to know someone who can get that done. In fact, if you're listening today, please know those are the magical eight words: *I know someone that can get that done.*"

"I really got into networking, and attempted to become useful and resourceful to many people, and you do that by just knowing people. Building networks, Cami, as you know, is an asset. When you have an asset like connecting to people, whether it's online or offline, you've got to nurture it, you got to share it, you've got to maintain it. Networking is not something you do just sometimes and some places. It's something, I believe, we can do all the time and everywhere. I got into it in the '70's. In the '80's, I began the expansion for the largest business networking program in the world. I think many people may know of it as BNI. In those days, we were known as the Networking California, and I began that expansion. Currently, I'm on the national expansion team for Goldstar referral clubs. They're in about 100 locations in 15 states. To me, it was always just getting together with people, and building a network—a system of elements. People that link together, I think, we all have the same in mind. We always want to expand our sphere of influence."

"We want to create opportunities for one another, and we want to gain access to information when we need it. For me, Cami, that's really what that's all about. Again, I have so much I can share about it, but to me, the most important thing is, I love people and I believe we're better together. I believe that the desire for success hasn't changed. What's changing, is how we get there, and all I know is this, Cami: If I help you, it makes it easier for you to want to help me. If we help one another, we all do better as a result. In fact, everybody listen, most relationships are built in some form of reciprocity. Networking is simply the sharing of ideas, information, and resources. You know, Cami, if I go to lunch with you at a meeting and we're sitting there and I say, I'm buying, you would probably fight with me or you would say, okay I'll buy next time. You see, most relationships are built in some form of reciprocity. It's equity and exchange. The question is, if you're reading this interview, think about and answer this question: What are you bringing to the table?"

"If you think it's just you, you're missing the boat. When I can leverage the many thousands of people I speak in front of, or the many thousands of people I'm connected to—whether it's Facebook or LinkedIn—when I can leverage that network to support others, I don't know, Cami, it doesn't get any better than that. Does it?"

Cami Baker:
"I love all the words that you're using, Ron. Leveraging and the law of reciprocity. I talk about the law of reciprocity all the

time. I tell people, *Hey, listen, the reason I even have a business card is because of what the law of reciprocity says, when I hand you something, you want to reciprocate and hand me something back.* I'm clear that if there's going to be any follow-up, it's usually 99% of the time from me, and a lot of time people don't follow-up. Ron, please enlighten me about what you've learned, because anyone who puts together BNI and Goldstar, clearly has this thing down. For me, the thousands and thousands of events, and the tens of thousands of people and business cards I see exchanged, the follow-up is an epidemic of people just having a hard time with following-up. I believe that one of the reasons why people have a hard time following-up, is because they try to get too many cards."

"They need to go for quality over quantity, that way they can go to an event and be more interested in two or three people, as opposed to twenty or thirty cards. Like you said, network with people and don't be a card collector, then the follow-up just comes naturally. You and I followed-up, we haven't even actually met face to face, but we were introduced, we got on the phone, we followed-up, and we continued a conversation. But, don't you find, most people don't follow up because they just get overwhelmed with so many cards, and they don't know what to do with them?"

Ron Sukenick:
"Yeah. Here's what happens, Cami. You said many great things—great nuggets—and I want to recapture those nuggets. First-of-all, most people love the joy of interaction. Increased interaction brings us increased cooperation. Repetition is what builds the reputation. First-of-all, most people in this world of networking, think that it's something you do sometimes and some places. They think it's a place you go to. You, and I know,

it's a place you can come from. Most people (and I say most people, meaning a large percentage of people), confuse activity for accomplishment. They think it's all about shaking hands and passing business cards. In fact, another thing you talked about, was to become interested in people. When you go to an event—here's a great nugget—when you go to any event, don't try to get people interested in you. My suggestion is you become the most *interested* person in the world."

Cami Baker:

"Amen!"

Ron Sukenick:

"Let's face it, networking is awkward, it's hit and miss at the situation, it always lacks support, and most people don't care about you. I'm talking to the audience right now. Most people, they're more interested in themselves."

Cami Baker:

"Of course, they are! I love what you're saying, because I say this stuff too."

Ron Sukenick:

"We all say it, right? I always tell people, just go out and become the most interested person in the room. Don't try to get people interested in you, because here's what happens: It automatically creates a desire in people to be interested in who you are. That's where you want to get people. Number two, you talk about follow-up."

"Let me give everybody a great nugget. I've tested this time, and time again, and I call it the magic of six. Here's the premise. If you can get up to six interactions with anybody, it is likely, you will have a great beginning for a relationship that will never end. Here's how it works. You meet somebody at an event. That's your first interaction. Then I'm always telling people to follow-up. See you got to put a system in place. Some of the best friends, some of the best connections I've ever made, Cami, in my life, are people I had met somewhere for the first time."

"If I meet you, Cami, and trust me, I would meet you, because when I look at your work and the stuff you're doing and your picture, who would not want to meet you, right? I know I'm just being truthful, but you and I would get along really well. It's not a matter of, well maybe Cami is a successful real estate broker or agent, or this or that. If I thought that was the limit to who you were, I'd be making a mistake, because we could all gain access to people; but, the biggest investment you'll have to make, is time. You must invest time in people. So, getting back to your follow-up discussion. If I send you an email within 24 hours or less, it will get your attention. Think about it everybody. You ever go to an event, and meet ten or fifteen interesting people? How many of those people are following-up with you? I bet you're going to tell me, maybe one or two, and here's the distinction. Most people don't follow-up because they're going after the sale."

"I always want people to go after this thing called: the relationship. See, if I can get to six interactions, it's likely I can have a good relationship with anyone. For the reading audience, if they send me an email at RS@RonSukenick.com, I will send you the article, or you can go to my website www.RonSukenick.com, and you can read about that magic of six. I always go after six interactions, and you and I, right now, Cami, are probably up to number four, maybe five. When we get to six, we have a great beginning for this relationship that will probably never end."

Cami Baker:

"That is so beautiful, and I love that you even say the nuggets; because, any time I go to any event I always get a great nugget. I'll give you an example. Last night, I went to an event in Boston, and the people who put on the event, were expecting about 100 people, and there were only about eight or ten of us there. It turned out to be so wonderfully delicious, Ron, because I got a chance to really spend some quality time with the two leaders who I really wanted to talk to, anyway, because as you just said, I've had several interactions with them, and we're definitely at number six by now. It was just time to have some good quality human, bridging the gap interaction conversation. It wasn't about going to meet 100 people. It was about talking to those two people and building that relationship. Frankly, my first thought was, *Oh there's not many people here*. On my way home, I did a video about it and I thought, *Wow, what a blessing that was that there wasn't a lot of people there*."

"I had a chance to really just have their undivided attention and build that relationship. This is why I say to people all the time, don't try to leave with twenty or thirty cards. Instead, talk to three to five people who will remember you. Those are the ones who you found interesting, and they found you interesting. I love what you said about the whole interesting part. People are so worried about what to say. Frankly, the less you say the more you make. The more of an impact you make, the more friends you make. The less you say, the more you make money, and the more you make connections. It's better to say less. Less is more. Right?"

133

Ron Sukenick:

"It is. Think about what you're saying. If you have ten people in a room, it's safe to say, most of those people know at least two to 300 people each. I'm sure our reading audience understands, that two to 300 times 10, sounds like maybe I'm gaining access to 20 to 3,000 people. Here's what's interesting. Some are thinking, *Wow, that would be plenty of people to gain access to. How do I get to them?* The only way you can get to them is, you must invest time in people. To me, that's really the biggest investment we make. We invest time in people. Again, I repeat what I said earlier. I don't know that I had any success in my life without the help of people. Look, here's what's truthful. Social capital in the country is way down. Social capital is defined as, the glue that keeps communities together. When I say it's way down Cami, what I mean is, some of our people who are reading, recognize that church attendance is down, club participation is down."

"In fact, there was a book called *Bowling Alone, by Robert Putnam,* that actually talked about, how there's a larger percentage of people who are bowling outside of leagues than in a league, and in fact, leagues can become extinct. Do you know what happens when social capital is weighed down? People are vulnerable, they're open. People are open, and right now, you and I are talking out in the month of September of 2016, and I will tell everybody, that there's been no better time in history, than right now, to get better connected to people. The question is, what can you do to become useful and resourceful? Keep nurturing, keep building, and keep strengthening your relationships. Go after the relationship. When people don't follow-up, they're going after the sale, but when they do follow-up, they're going after the relationship. If I'm going to an event trying to figure out what you can do for me, I'm going after the sale. When I go to an event looking out for what I can do for you, I'm going after the relationship. To me that's really what it's all about."

"By the way, in 2004, my second book was titled *The Power Is in The Connection*. It was built around a philosophy called, net-being, which is a word that captures the essence of a relationship mindset, and all I said was: "*You have to be, before you can do.*" You do to the extent of who you are, and who you are is based predominantly on how you think. The key to success, accomplishments, and power, is our ability to BE."

"E.E. Cummings is an American poet who stated, *you can teach almost anybody to think, believe, and know; but, it's difficult to teach anybody to be.* The only other comment I'll make, because I've taken up so much time with you, but it's been fun, is this thing about listening. Here's the question to the reading audience: When was the last time anybody said, *Thanks for taking the time to listen?* Has it been a while? I'll tell you what's so important, and I know you know this Cami. When I speak, I learn what I know, when I listen, I learn what you know."

"*What gives us competitive advantage in the marketplace, is our ability to listen; because, if we're a leader and we don't listen, we eventually are surrounded by people who have nothing to say.* Unbelievable quote! I got that from Andy Stanley. I wish I had made that up myself. Let me say that one last time. *If you're not listening to people, you're eventually surrounded by those who have nothing to say.* I don't know that it gets any better than that; but, listen, we're only here for a short period-of-time. Why do I have to wait forever to build relationships, when I can build them right now, right at the point of interaction."

"That's what I go after Cami, and I'm thrilled to have met Mary, who had thought that maybe we should get connected. I immediately figured out who you were, we were immediately on the phone communicating. I got to come out there! You and I got to team up Cami, we got to do something!"

Cami Baker:

"Yes, we do need to do something together, and it has been my honor to have you on the phone! I am glad that I recorded this, so that I can go back and listen to it, and I love what you're saying about listening. I tell people all the time when they say, *Hey, what do you do?* that they must stop. It's that same old question we hear all the time. I say to them: "*You know what? I know what I do, and if I'm talking I'm not learning. Tell me about you.*"

Ron Sukenick:

"Can I make one last comment? I want to suggest to everybody, or bring to their attention that Microsoft did spend, $26,200,000,000 about three months ago to buy LinkedIn. I'm suggesting to everybody to embrace the power of LinkedIn. You've got to, because you're either LinkedIn or you're linked out. You can go from high tech, like on LinkedIn, to high touch, and end up at some restaurant or some coffee shop. Whether it's a Starbucks or a Panera Bread, or whatever is in your area. You got to embrace the power of LinkedIn. If anybody is interested in anything to do with my work, Cami, they can certainly go to RonSukenick.com. That's one location, and of course I gave my email address, RS@RonSukenick.com. Any friends of yours, is certainly, going to be a friend of mine."

Cami Baker:

"I look forward to learning more from you about LinkedIn; because, it is definitely one of the platforms that I have not learned a lot about. I have said many times: "*Social media makes us the most anti-social people on the planet.*" I find it ironic that they call it social media, when like you said, people have stopped belonging to clubs and going to church, and it does make us vulnerable and/or open and susceptible."

"One of our basic human needs besides food, water, and shelter, is the touch of another human being. In one form or another we strive for, we long for, we live for community, and the fact that the community has gotten so big and yet so small at the same time, is very ironic. You and I can go on and on forever Ron, and we will, and when you come to Boston we're going to do a ginormous, beautiful, lovely event. Even if it's just the two of us at a Panera."

Ron Sukenick:
"You know you touch on so many great things. You just talked about John Bowlby, who is a psychologist, who talked about the theory of attachment. We're going to have to get into that another time. The theory of attachment. That's when we're born. Remember, we come out and we're attached to something, and we're always attached to the mom for safety and for comfort, and for food and survival. We'll talk about that; but, I'll be out there. When I get close, Cami, you can count on me connecting with you."

Cami Baker:
"Awesome my friend. Thank you for your time, and anyone who is reading...there are nuggets in here that, won't just enhance your impact and income as you network, but from my perspective of being a lifelong student of growth, will help you grow as a human being too. Ron, it has been my privilege, and my honor. I do consider you friend, and hey, all I can say is,

thank you so much for your time."

Ron Sukenick:

"Thank you so much! Look forward to speaking again. Cami, have a great day!"

CONVERSATION WITH
DIANE REYNOLDS

Cami Baker:

"Hi, this is Cami Baker. I'm on the phone with Diane Reynolds, and we are talking about, coaching and mentoring from a seasoned business woman's perspective. Diane, would you please share with our readers, what it was, that as a seasoned businesswoman, had you wanting to be open to coaching in the first place."

Diane Reynolds:

"I'm always open to coaching and learning every day and every moment. I always think it's important, to have a mentor and a coach. Professional athletes have mentors and coaches, and their performances on the field, just keep getting better and better. I feel that's what I need in my business life as well."

Cami Baker:

"Awesome, I totally agree. I have had a coach-mentor situation with multiple coaches at one time. Actually, since I was in my early 30s, starting out in real estate. So, I totally respect that, and hear that. Now, when you started looking for a coach and/or mentor, what were you looking for? What were the qualities or characteristics you wanted?"

Diane Reynolds:

"Well, I was really looking for a coach that had similar philosophies to other mentors that I have had. Not as a close relationship, but people like Mike Ferry. So, I was looking for someone who was along the same vein, that had the same philosophies, and were for top producers. These types of coaches would be ones who, keep us on top of our game; and quite frankly, needed to be someone in the area who I could have easy access to. I know we have technology, and all those things, but I really made a decision that I wanted to go with you, Cami; because you're very accessible, and you know exactly what I need. I really want to be you when I grow up."

Cami Baker:

"Yes, we have been able to reach out, and even hug on occasion when I've done different venues. You definitely come out to participate; and you and I both know, we have a relationship as a real estate coach and client. However, we also cover more of a business, networking, and general people skills. Tell me, what were some of the specific things that you wanted to accomplish, when we started our relationship?"

Diane Reynolds:

"In the sales arena, I know the importance of consistency, schedules, staying on track, staying focused, being in the moment, remaining professional, and all of those traits that we need to have in this professional sales environment. So, I was fortunate enough to be able to be reminded, during our coaching sessions, about all those things. You reminded me about the consistency, staying on track, staying on schedule, remaining professional in my presentations, in my voice, and in my tonality; as well as remaining calm, cool, and collected. I was looking to further all those skills that it takes in our top producing sales environment. I just wanted to keep getting them sharper and sharper."

Cami Baker:

"I really applaud you on that, because I can hear a really nice improvement in your voice, even today. Not that there was anything wrong with your voice, but you're just keeping it more at a tone that is professional and level; yet expressive. So, great job on that! Now, when we first started talking to one another, I'm sure there were some levels of you wanting to learn scripts and objection handling and all that; but, what I loved about all of our conversations, was how they always took on a life of their own. In the end, we both always ended up getting something from the call, that we weren't expecting. Tell me a couple of the key factors that, have really changed your mindset or enhanced the way you do business, outside of what you thought you were going to get in our relationship."

Diane Reynolds:

"That would be some of the intangible things. So, my skills are one thing. But, some of the things that I wasn't expecting were, the mindset issues that you and I talked about at length. I believe nearly every one of our calls, we talked about mindset; and because of this, I have come miles from where I was. My mindset has shifted to the approach of serving my clients and coming from that perspective all the time. I know that it's important. I've seen it."

Cami Baker:

"I love that you say that, and you know that mindset is so important. Let's face it, everything starts in our mind. Every building that's built, every book that's written, every piece of clothing, every piece of furniture, everything in our life, was created in somebody's mind before it manifested. So, I personally focus on that too. I ask myself: *Where is my mindset? What am I thinking? How am I feeling about this person I'm getting ready to call, or this event I'm getting ready to walk into?* Because, how I feel, is going to come out massively, before I even walk in the door or pick up that phone."

"Just as a last little minute tidbit, what kind of advice would you give to someone who is in business, and wanting to shorten their learning curve, and double, triple, quadruple their efforts in a short period-of-time? Especially centered around mentoring and coaching, because you seem to be really open to that. What kind of advice would you give that person?"

Diane Reynolds:
"I would say: "*Be open.*" I would say: "*No matter what your skill levels are, they can be sharpened.*" All of them. I would also tell them to: "*Keep going.*" I really believe, now in our relationship, that the mindset was the key for me. It unlocked a lot. But, it just seems, that once you have a handle on your mindset, the possibilities just open-up, and it just brings a whole new perspective. So, for my opinion, get the coaching and mentoring regarding mindset. Never mind the skills. The foundation that I've built, and the confidence, are skills that I wanted to work on. That aside, really the mindset was huge for me personally. So, I would say to others, to look at their mindset intently, in addition to their skills development."

Cami Baker:
"I know you said that it was important for you, but I really want to instill, with anyone reading this, that the mindset is where it all starts for everyone. Frankly, if your mindset is, *I already know everything I need to know*, you're probably the person who needs to know more, because that's never true. I know I say all the time: "*The more I know, the more I know I need to know, and the more I know I don't know.*"

Diane Reynolds:
"Again, I just want to stress, the skills and the skills development was what I initially went in for. Then, it became

something totally different, as I worked through that process. It really was about the mindset. It starts and ends with the mindset, and the mindset unlocked all that stuff in the middle for me. So, thank you Cami."

Cami Baker:

"Thank you, Diane. I look forward to seeing you at the upcoming event in a couple of weeks, and for many more events for years to come. I consider you my friend. You have a great day."

Diane Reynolds:

"Me too. Thank you. Have a great day, Cami."

CONVERSATION WITH JOHN MELTON

Cami Baker:

"This is Cami Baker, from CamiBaker.com. I'm on the phone with one of my longtime contacts, John Melton. Yes, the real John Melton, and that's his website, www.RealJohnMelton.com."

"I have known John for many many years, and we actually, worked in the same company a long time ago. John is a professional polished perfect example of the prospector and/or networker—or as I like to say, netWebber. He has really been able to take networking to a different level, and make it fun and play with it, just like I talk about doing. Let's take the work out of networking, and let's play our way through creating our NetWeb."

"John, I would love for you to share with our readers in this book, a little bit about networking, how you got started creating your NetWeb, and just where you started, and just the whole fun story about, how you got to where you are today."

John Melton:

"Absolutely, Cami. I really appreciate the awesome introduction, and I'm excited to be here. For me, I got started as an entrepreneur 15 years ago. I would say, over the last several years, we've definitely taken our entrepreneurial skill set to the internet. The internet has been so effective for us to build up our brand—to build our netweb."

"They say, your network will determine your net worth in a lot of cases, because if you build up a large database of fans, followers, friends, and amazing people like yourself, it's just inevitable, that you're going to build something that will be lucrative—something that should be fun. Look, if you don't like what you do, if you're not having fun, then you should do something else. I know that my mentor, years and years ago, used to say, *If you're not having fun, you're doing it wrong.*"

"I really do love, how you've taken networking and turned it into netwebbing; because networking, when you think about it, it doesn't sound like a fun or strategic activity, because you're working. I really believe if someone loves what they do, it doesn't feel like work. It shouldn't seem like work."

"People will say to me, *Well, John, you work all the time.* I'm like, *Well, I love what I do, so I want to do it all the time.* Being a stay at home dad, being able to support my family, and that's not just my kids and my wife. My wife and I work together, we're business partners and best friends. In fact, you know we've been married for over a decade now. Ultimately, we support her parents, and my mom financially. Believe it or not, they all have moved into our house."

"At the end of the day, it's amazing what we've been able to create because of that netweb, because we've developed these relationships over time. A lot of these relationships have actually become great friendships. That's what it's all about."

Cami Baker:
"I love how you say that. I've been saying that relationship is revenue that rocks. To be able to form those relationships, I tell people, *Stop looking for weeds, and start planting your seeds.* I mean, I was speaking the other day, and I asked the group: *"Who here, by a show of hands, wants to be somebody's lead?"* No one raised their hand, because of course they weren't thinking, *Oh,*

I'm going to go out today and I hope somebody puts me on their hit list—on their lead list. Let's stop looking at people as leads and start looking at them as human beings just like us and creating those relationships. It's kind of funny that social media has made us, in some cases, the most antisocial people."

"We have all these tools at our disposal, and some people use them very properly, which would be you and your beautiful wife. So, share with us about, how you've taken netwebbing from just being out grabbing cards and calling people, and doing the face to face, and also just taking it into social media, and really being able to brand yourself, and put it to a place where you're making $50,000+ a month."

John Melton:

"I could tell you this: It's great to build relationships, it's great to meet people, it's obviously crucial if you want to monetize your brand online and put out valuable content. That's one thing we've learned from Gary Vaynerchuk, and other online entrepreneurs and trainers. They all say, and teach, the same thing: You need to teach if you want to sell. If you out-teach your competition, it's inevitable, that over a period-of-time, people will start to look at you as an expert. The more you're educating, the more you're teaching, the more content you're putting out into the marketplace, like you're doing right now, whoever is reading this is going, *Wow, this is some good stuff, this is some good content?*"

"They'll start looking at your channel; whether it's a TV channel, radio channel, podcast, Facebook, Snapchat, or Instagram. They start looking at your channel, as a value-based channel, versus like most online entrepreneurs who are wannabes, and who have more of an infomercial channel. All they're trying to do is sell, sell, sell, pitch, pitch, pitch. If you ever pick up the book that Gary Vaynerchuk wrote, *Jab, Jab, Jab, Right Hook*, that's what it's all about. Value, value, value, and then, oh, by the way, for those of you who want to dive deeper, I have this online program, or, I have this coaching course, or I have a book that you can pick up. Whatever that looks like."

"The point is, if you want to build a large following, then you need to learn to teach. It doesn't mean that you're the end all, be all, expert on it. None of us are on everything. But, you can literally teach what it is you're learning. Say you pick *Think and Grow Rich by Napoleon Hill*, you read the book, you learn some great takeaways, so you record a video and upload it to Facebook or YouTube to get yourself out there. Talk about what you're implementing, and what's working for you. It's just a matter of taking people with you on this thing we call life. We have this life we're living, this journey we're on. Take people with you."

Cami Baker:
"That's a great point, and to that point, not only, are you and I giving it our best effort to give people great content and teach, but for me, and it sounds like for you too John, the more I teach, and the more I become a student, the more I want to learn. I've been saying this for years: *"The more I know, the more I know I don't know, and the more I know I need to know."* The more that I want to give out, the more I realize that I start to become a sponge and bring it in. It's almost like I'm a mama bird going out and getting the worm and wanting to go give it to the baby birds. Like, *Hey, look, here's something that I found, and here's something that's yummy that you might want to chew on and see."*

148

"The more we teach, the more we become a good student, the more we become a more expanded human being, the more opportunities come to us, and the more people want what we have in our life."

"Let me just say, surrounding ourselves with the right mindset, or the people who are like-minded, has absolutely changed my life. Can you speak on mentorship, coaching, and how if that has—and I know that it has for you—been a benefit for you, and changing or expanding you as a person?"

John Melton:
"Well, I think ultimately, all of us start somewhere, and that's the one thing, I have to talk people off the ledge about a lot. They're so hung up on their past and their circumstances, and none of that really matters. I know it might matter, in the sense that it matters to you, and it matters in the grand scheme of things, but it doesn't matter moving forward. Meaning, all the baggage that I brought with me into this marketing space, was just holding me back, so the better I've gotten at releasing that fear, that hesitation, and that past history, like, *Oh well, I'm not really good at public speaking*, or *I don't have any experience with selling or training or other people.* All of that nonsense is only in my head, and even if some of it was true to an extent, all of this is learnable."

"The personal development that we've plugged into over the years—having mentors and investing in ourselves—people say, *Well, what do you want to invest in? What's the best investment?* I mean, yea, real estate, the stock market, all that stuff sounds great, but if you invest in yourself, in your education, your skill set, your mindset, your philosophy, and you invest in other people, then that in turn, invests in you. That's the best

149

investment you can make. Any guru, any expert, any speaker, trainer, any successful person will tell you—it's their education, it's their experience, it's what they were willing to invest in themselves that made them who they are today. I can definitely say that that's true."

Cami Baker:
"I love what you said, because I've been saying lately, that it's important to look at our mindset, before we look at the skill set. People ask me all the time: *"What do you say when somebody says this? How do you introduce yourself to a stranger? How do you give a good first impression at a networking event? How do you follow up with people?"* They're looking for the skill set, and that's all very important, and as you just said, it's a learned skill. However, the mindset comes long before the skill set. You can have the best skill set in the world, but if your mindset is *you're never going to use it anyway* then it's all useless. Having said all that, you mentioned that you've had to talk people off the ledge."

"My listeners, my readers, my tribe, and my peeps are entrepreneurs, they're business owners, they're commission-based salespeople, and they're all heart centered and visionaries. Everyone who's reading this book, to some extent, is having sales conversations with people. Just to bring our conversation a little bit to a close, give us a couple of yummy good juicy nuggets on when you're talking to someone and you're *having to talk them off a ledge.* I know I've done that many times myself. What do you find to be the best way to help somebody understand, *Hey listen, I get that finances are tight, or you've got to ask permission from your husband, or the time is not right.* Whatever that mindset is, how do you help people get through that challenge, or do you?"

John Melton:

"I mean, I will definitely make recommendations. I'm certainly not going to beg anybody or convince anybody. I like to encourage and recommend, but there is a fine line between encouraging someone and convincing someone. I think we both know from our experience, when you convince somebody to spend money, when you convince somebody to join a business, or buy something they don't really need, they end up, number one, returning it a lot of times, they end up cancelling, so that's just a big headache, and ultimately you also start to turn people off. Maybe the timing isn't the best. Obviously, encourage and recommend, that's great, but if you come at them with *commission breath*, as I like to call it, and you're clearly looking at them as a dollar sign and not a human, and you're not listening to their needs, you're not really doing what's in their best interests. You're just trying to make you money, and it's going to hurt you in the long-run."

Cami Baker:

"I love that. I've never heard of *commission breath*, but that is so appropriate. I can really relate to that. Having had that breath in the past, and having had it spewed on me, I can definitely relate to that."

John Melton:

"Yea, we've all been there."

Cami Baker:

"I teach my people. I coach, I mentor, I suggest, I highly recommend lots and lots, and I've got a couple of hundred simple tips, all the way to advanced tips, on how to be a better networker. I put together a system called *The New Rules of Networking*, and the way that I explain it to people is this: We are all—every human being that's breathing—looking for income, influence, and/or impact in one way or another. If they want to change the world and have a big impact, they'd better have some influence—and a little bit of bank behind them doesn't hurt—and it all starts, how, if, and when they are communicating, how they are conversating, and where they seem to drop the ball. You need to communicate, conversate, collaborate, to create all of those things."

"With that in mind, knowing that we met out in the hungry field of networking—long before we understood it was actually netwebbing—what are a couple of juicy little tips you can give the reader, from your experience, that has helped your tribe to become better communicators, conversators, and collaborators?"

John Melton:
"Such a great question. I think there is a lot of value in getting people to pay, because when they pay they pay attention. We run some virtual workshops, we have different programs and courses that we recommend. Again, we'll put out free content. A lot of your free content, should revolve around, the what you know, what you do here, and what you do there. If they want to learn the how to do it, typically that'll cost money. I notice that if people want to improve, the ones that typically do, aren't just looking to improve, but they're also the ones that put their money where their mouth is. Like I said earlier, investing in yourself is huge, and what that means is, investing in the courses and in the programs. If there's a virtual workshop or a live seminar, or a bootcamp…you gotta plug in…you gotta get around the right people, and you have to implement."

"It's really easy to listen to an audiobook or a podcast, or buy a course and listen to it, and then say, *Yea, I'm going to do that, I might do this, and that sounds good and that sounds great.* They get overwhelmed, they get inundated, and they start to make things a lot more difficult than they need to be. It's just like, *Dude, just take action. Just implement one thing at a time, get good at it, have long term vision, and improve your skill set over time.* You know what, it's sometimes good to get some feedback. Maybe hire a coach. Someone like yourself, Cami. Right? Hire someone who is a great communicator. They are great at collaborating, they know how to build a network, they've made money, and they know how to communicate. If you hire an expert who can help you, or you at least invest in a course, a book, or a program, you will pay attention because you've paid. Stop searching on YouTube for all the answers because when something is free you get what you pay for, and when something is expensive you get what you pay for. Right?"

"Again, I know there are examples on both sides of the spectrum, where somebody will say, *Wow, I had this very fortunate situation where I got to learn from this one gal, and she did it for free.* Or, *Oh, hey, I paid thousands and thousands of dollars for a program and I got nothing out of it.* I'm sure there are examples of both, but for the most part, when you invest in yourself, you're better off than the people who are looking for free handouts. Again, it's not bad to learn from the free content in the world. I'm telling you to create free content to attract leads and to attract people to you, but in the grand scheme of things, if somebody really wants to improve, and they don't want to wait ten, fifteen, or twenty years to figure it out on their own, then if you want to speed up the process you've got to be willing to invest in yourself, and typically, when we invest in ourselves, Cami, it comes back ten times."

Cami Baker:

"It sure does. I've heard it put this way, John, when it comes to commitment, there are people who are interested and there are people who want to be informed. They get a little bit of information, then they get involved. Maybe they're following you on Facebook, maybe they're getting that free content. They get immersed, maybe they get a CD or something and they listen to it in their car, but then they get invested. If they're just interested or just informed, they're really not taking the steps. When they start to get involved, get immersed, it's like you just said. When they jump in and are invested, that's a whole different ball game. It's so telling, that we were all sold on, spending tens or hundreds of thousands of dollars on an education for an occupation, and then when we get out of college, we can't even get a job."

"I know a lot of extremely educated people, who work menial jobs, because they couldn't even get hired in their chosen field. Why people will spend tens or hundreds of thousands on a formal education, when self-education will make them millions, I have no idea. But you're right, the idea does get lost in there. I'm just so thrilled that we've had this beautiful conversation, and that I'm able to share it with thousands of people, with my community, your community, and the like."

"This is just a perfect example, of two people who were able to communicate and shake hands many years ago, pass each other in the hallway in a different business, and have a couple of friendly conversations; but guys, the seed was planted. If John and had I looked at each other as lead, lead, lead, we never would have stayed in contact, because we were already in the same company and we weren't a lead for each other. However, years later a little bit of planting the seed, a little bit of follow-up, a little bit of, as John said, free content. I've been watching him. I've been watching him grow, and he's been making, *Hey, kudos to you, Cami,* comments to me. We've been supporting each other. Here we are today having a beautiful collaboration, which I hope inspires. I'm already inspired myself, but I want to be inspiring, and inspire others to do the same thing."

"Guys, let's collaborate, let's not compete. Don't worry about your competition. Let the competition worry about you. And really, there is no such thing as competition. When you shift your mind to collaboration over competition, the world is your oyster. John Melton, would you please give our audience your website, your Facebook, your cell phone, how they can send you a smoke signal, and send a carrier pigeon...whatever it is that you want them to have in order to get in touch with you, because you are one powerful human being."

John Melton:
"Thank you. Well, first-of-all, I definitely appreciate our conversation. Second-of-all, if somebody wants to find me on any social media platform, Snapchat, Instagram, Facebook, just go to Real John Melton, or search *Real John Melton* on any one of those social medial platforms, and you'll be able to find me. My website is www.RealJohnMelton.com."

Cami Baker:
"Imagine that. See guys, when you brand yourself, it's pretty simple. Look at that, it all just matches, and one of the great things about branding ourselves is that, John Melton, will always be John Melton. It doesn't matter what company he's affiliated with, it doesn't matter any of the other brands or

whatever, he will always be John Melton. It is so beautiful that people are learning to brand themselves, which John is an expert at. If you'd like to get better branded, reach out to John. John, it's been my honor, my friend. We will talk soon. By the way, when I'm heading between Boston and Miami over the next six months or so, I'd love to stop in; and if you and your wife are doing any events, I can help teach the new rules of NetWebbing."

John Melton:
"I love it."

Cami Baker:
"Have a great day."

John Melton:
"All right, awesome, thank you."

PART 5
BONUS MATERIAL

IN CLOSING

Now that we've come to the end of this book, I want to make sure, you create your creed. I'll give you the creed next, along with, a list of different techniques to think about before you go to your next networking event. The creed and the techniques will help you to set the right intention, pay attention, and have the retention of your resources, relationships, and revenue.

In life, we pay a price for everything. For example, by purchasing this book, you purchased knowledge. It's not about the price you paid; rather it's the value of your time that you invested in educating and applying what you learn. Moreover, the real question is: *Is the price you're paying an investment, or is it a cost—an expense?* When you choose to apply what you have learned in this book, it becomes an investment. You invested in your future—in your success. If you poorly choose to not apply what you have learned, then yes, it is a cost—an expense.

Think about it. When we pay for anything in life, whether it be $50 to attend an event, or $500 for a plane ticket, we are either spending or investing. I encourage you to see the dollar sign as an investment in your future. Answer the following questions: Are you looking at expenses as an investment in your education? Your business? Your increasing resource list? Or, are you saying statements such as, "Well, what's it going to cost me?"

If someone says to me, "Cami, what's it going to cost me to work with you?" My question to them is, "What is it costing you not to?" When it comes to business, thinking from a perspective of, *what's it going to cost me*, is a hindering mindset. Stop asking that question. Don't think of an opportunity as a, *what's it going to cost me* situation. Instead, ask yourself, and think in terms of, *What's the investment, and how is it going to pay off?* A well-educated and savvy business person, considers their ROI—Return On Investment.

THE CREED

Let's talk about the creed. In a moment, we are going to make the creed. However, let me first, preface it; because, I want to make sure that you fully understand it. When you are at a networking event, and someone puts a card in your hand, there is no contractual obligation. There are no rules that say, "Oh, because you gave me a card, I'm supposed to, and I have to, follow-up with you." Those cards that are shoved in your hand, are not worth the paper they're printed on. The person who put it in your hand, is just spraying and praying, and that doesn't have anything to do with you.

Also, if people ask you for your card, you don't have to ask them for a card back in return. As a matter-of-fact, unless you see a possible relationship, and plan to follow-up with them, you shouldn't ask for one back.

The creed we are about to create, is about when you are asking for a business card—when you walk up to someone and are having a little chit chat. You come to the place in the conversation where you ask, "Hey, can I have your business card?" Or, "Wow! That's interesting. Let me get your contact information, and I'll follow-up." When you ask for a card, you should only ask for it because, you have full intention of following-up, and you will follow-up within one week.

The fact is, to ask for someone's card and not follow-up, shows a lack of integrity; and basically, it's a lie. It's like a guy asking a girl for her phone number. She gives it to him, and then he never calls her. (She'll be pretty upset about that.)

Do not ask for cards, unless, you have full intentions of calling them. Here's the deal: People who go around collecting cards (being a card collector), create a misconception. They think they've gone out networking, obtained leads, and that there's business coming in. When in fact, none of that is true.

So, what's the creed? It may be a bit different for each person; however, it goes something like this:

"I, <state your name>, *solemnly swear, to never ever ask for a business card again; unless, I have full intentions to follow-up. When I follow-up, I will follow-up within one week.*"

Back to the disclaimer from earlier in the book. You can exchange the word "card" with "contact". If you are not actually giving/taking physical business cards in lieu of an electronic version, do not be confused. *You are still asking for contact information, and should not do it, unless you plan to actually contact them.* Imagine that...a contact is for contacting!

Now, a follow-up means something personal. Whether it be a phone call, email, or other platform it should be personal; and, no, I'm not talking about a bulk email to 28 people, who were: *so nice to meet you,* at the event. Also, I'm not talking about, simply friending them on Facebook or LinkedIn, and then thinking, somewhere along the line, they're going to write you a $10,000 check.

I'm talking about, reaching out and making it personal.

Make it about them. This way they know you were listening, and that you care. It's about creating Resources, Relationships, and Revenue. Resources of people who can help you out, who can hook you up, who can be of some sort of assistance to you, and who you can reciprocate, in order to build relationships that lead to revenue.

When you create your creed, you are saying you are ready to step out, step up, step in, and take on creating your NetWeb. You are committed to being a relationship creator. You are ready to be genuine, authentic, and a (wo)man of your word.

It is my educated guess that, you want people to be able to trust you. Well, if I am correct about this, then it is essential for you to stick by your creed. Once you do, people will think, "(Your Name), asked for my card and actually followed-up. Wow! I can do business with a person like that. I can trust this person to keep their word. When this person says they're going to do something, they do it. All the while, Bill asked me for a card, and I never heard from him. Also, I saw him at another event, and he asked me for another card. Now I'm on his email list. What's that?"

Remember, be certain, you are being received and perceived in the light in which you would like to be.

The Creed

"I, _____,
solemnly swear,
to never ever ask for a
business card again; unless,
I have full intentions to follow-up.
When I follow-up,
I will follow-up within one week."

Mingle to Millions

The Art and Science of Building Business
Relationships and Mastering Referrals.

YOUR CHEAT SHEET

Here we are at the cheat sheet, the checklist, and the bullet points that you may want to review when you're considering going to an event. Also, you will find it beneficial to review these before you go to an event. Remember, we as efficient, effective, professional, productive, and profitable netwebbers, want to Research, Reach out, and Relationship build; and we want to do all of this before we even go to an event. As a matter-of-fact, *the before* is a big part of the event. From now on, consider *the before* as part of going to the event.

1. Find out who is going to the event.

Do research and reach out to the people who you know are attending the event and begin the process of building a relationship with each of them. I call this "Research, Reach out, Relationship build...the 3 R's. Create a relationship via E-mail, Facebook, a phone call, Skype (whatever platform works for you). Be sure to not just introduce yourself; but, start a conversation. Ask them a relationship building question. Something I like to ask is, "So tell me, what do you love about networking?"

Another key element to keep in mind, is to be sure at the end of the first Reach out, have a call to action. Don't just say, "Hey Jeff, I look forward to seeing you at the event."

Rather say, "Hey Jeff, I look forward to seeing you at the event. If I get there before you, I will save you a seat. Do you need one seat or two saved?"

The above is just an example of what I might use. You may decide to say something else; either way, ask an open-ended question. Asking questions and having a call to action, is going to help get the banter going between you and them. This is how you build a relationship. So, that's your first step: Research, Reach Out, and Relationship Build.

2. Arrive at the event early.

When you arrive early to an event, you will find there are many advantages. First, you can help prepare for the event by passing out literature, set up the chairs, or place the waters on the tables. While you are helping, you can be engaging with the people in charge of putting on the event. The people putting the event on, are the movers and shakers. They are connected. Start *mingling your way to millions.*

3. Be the unofficial ambassador.

As you begin to meet people, begin introducing people to each other. The law of reciprocity says, *when you do something for me, I naturally want to do something for you.* When you get there early enough, and you're meeting everybody as they're coming in, it's easier than you might think to introduce people to each other. Plus, you will find within five or ten minutes of doing this, all-of- a-sudden, those people are bringing people over to meet you. It's a beautiful thing.

4. Give a good first impression.

How do you feel about yourself? How do you feel

about your services? How you feel comes through in your body language. Your body is screaming at people before you even open your mouth. What is your body saying to other people? When you walk in the room, are you commanding presence, or are you just a wallflower? Are you just fading into the background? So, consider how you're being received and perceived, before you even speak.

5. Know what you're going to say.

How are you speaking? What are you going to say to people when you meet them? Please don't tell me you're going to walk up to somebody and ask, "What do you do?" Because, if that's all you've got, you need to go back and re-read this book. The fact is, this approach is boring and overused. You want to be bold. You want to be creative. You want to be memorable. You want to create relationships with people. You want to create a conversation that naturally flows into a beautiful follow-through, collaboration, business, and relationship. So, stop asking, "What do you do?" by having other alternatives like "What project are you working on?" There are lots of creative ways to start conversations. You can watch my videos on this, and a million other topics, on my YouTube Channel or other social media.

6. Focus on quality over quantity.

Play a little game with yourself: Only put five business cards in your pocket. This way, you are forced to be very selective about who you're giving them to. Keep in mind, nobody's going to call you anyway. Let's face it, the only reason you have the cards with you, is to get the other person's card when you give your card. Trust me, if you don't get their card, nothing is going to happen. So, limit yourself to a few cards, so you will remember to limit how many people you are spending time with at the event. Plus, if it's a one-hour event, you truly only have enough time, to truly get to know three to five people.

7. Take notes on the cards.

Quality versus Quantity. As you move forward through the event, make sure you put notes on the business cards you collect. Be sure to set yourself up for a follow-through. Are you having a conversation that leads you to, send them the link to that book you recommended? Or, the link to a restaurant, that based on your conversation, they would love? Or, did you get a physical address? If so, mail them a $25 gift card, a sample of your product, or just a simple *it was nice to meet you* card with a coupon inside.

8. Follow-up, right then-and-there.

As a matter-of-fact, as far as follow-through goes, set it up right then-and-there—on the spot. Get your calendar out and have them get their calendar out. Then say, "Great conversation! Let's finish this conversation. Is Monday at 4:00 p.m. or Tuesday at 3:00 p.m. better?" If you don't schedule it right then, there's a good chance of never getting that person on the phone. That's just life; but, if you get it scheduled, they're much more committed to following-through with you.

So, those are just a few tips I give away. Make sure that you put this list in your pocket, in your purse, and in your car. Be sure it is accessible to you on the fly—never leave home without it! Also, be sure to share it with those who you collaborate with, your friends, your family, and the stranger on the street. Let's get the world creating a NetWEB—so together, everyone wins!

If you are ever in the Boston area, be sure to attend my annual event, *Network on Fire*. As for now, I hold this event in the Boston area; but, as the Mingle to Millions brand continues to grow, you will see the *Network on Fire* event taking place across the nation. So, keep your eyes open and ears perked. And, of course, Mingle your way to Millions!

In conclusion, you want to: Attract your clients, customers, and audience. Build your credibility. Position yourself as the authority and expert in your marketplace. You can be as local, regional, national, or global as you desire to be. It starts with: *BEING THE EVENT.*

Whether you want to, *Be the Event*, by owning your power in your space at other people's events...or through creating your own events, let's have a conversation about how CamiBaker.com and the Mingle to Millions team can guide you to your version of ….BE THE EVENT!

Now go out and create your NetWeb!

CAMI RECOMMENDS

Spiritual/Motivational Specific:

Esther and Jerry Hicks

- Ask and It Is Given
- The Law of Attraction

Jim Rohn

- Anything Rohn does

W. Clement Stone

- Anything by Stone

John Maxwell

- Failing Forward
- Today Matters

Marcia Wieder

- Making Your Dreams Come True

Charlie "Tremendous" Jones

- Anything by Charlie

Deepak Chopra

- The Seven Spiritual
- Break Out Of The Box

Wayne Dyer

- The Power of Intention
- Real Magic

Linda Kaplan

- The Power of Nice

Wallace Wattles

- The Science of Getting Rich

T. Harv Ecker

- Secrets of the Millionaire Mind

Susan Jeffers

- Feel the Fear and Do it Anyway
- End the Struggle and Dance with Life.
- Excuse Me Your Life Is Waiting

Napoleon Hill

- Think and Grow Rich
- The Law of Success In 16 Lessons

Dale Carnegie

- How to Win Friends and Influence People
- How to Stop Worrying and Start Living

Louise Hay (www.HayHouse.com)

- You Can Heal Your Life

Hay House radio on internet

- "I Can Do It" seminars

Unknown

- As a Man Thinkith
- Hung By the Tongue

- The Tongue of Creative Force
- What You Say Is What You Get
- The Secret

Business Specific:

Robert Kiyosaki

- Rich Dad Poor Dad
- Cash Flow Quadriants
- All books in the Rich Dad/Poor Dad franchise

Donald Trump

- Why We Want You to Be Rich

Joel Moskowitz

- 10 16% Solution (Real Estate Tax Liens)

David Bach

- Smart Women Finish Rich

David Hawkins

- Power vs. Force

Mark Victor Hansen

- The One Minute Millionaire

Darren Hardy

- The Compound Effect

(Publisher of Success Magazine)

- Success Magazine

- Sign up for "Darren Dailey" texts

General Learning and Mind Expansion:

Price Pritchett

- You2 (you squared)

Og Mandino

- The Greatest Salesman in the World

Russell H Conwell

- Acres of Diamonds

Allan Pease

- Body Language (How to read other's thoughts by their gestures)

David J Schwartz

- The Magic of Thinking Big

Richard Branson

- Screw It, Let's Do It

Jeff Olson

- The Slight Edge

Unknown

- Psycho Cybernetics
- The Magic of Believing
- The Go Getter
- The Game of Work

Sales Specific:

Zig Ziglar

- See You at The Top
- Secrets of Closing the Sale
- (Anything by Zig)

Brian Tracy

- Eat That Frog

Seminars/Tapes/Books:

Tony Robbins (www.anthonyrobbins.com)

- "Unleash the Power Within" (This is the firewalking seminar)
- Personal Power

Landmark Education   (www.landmarkeducation.com)

- Landmark Forum (For kids and adults. Life changing.)

Vipassana Meditation Center   (www.dhara.dhamma.org)

- 10 Day Meditation in Shelburne, Ma
- Mike Ferry (www.mikeferry.com)
- Productivity School
- Action Workshop

Matthew Ferry (www.matthewferry.com)

- Sales Velocity
- NLP Training (Neuro Linguistic Programing, LOTS of books on this subject.)

Earl Knightinggale (www.nightingale-conant.com)

- Lead the Field
- The Strangest Secret

Dr Matt James (www.NLP.com)

Direct Marketing Specific:

Mark Yarnell

- Your First Year In Network Marketing

Richard Poe

- Wave 3 and Wave 4 book series

Allan Pease

- Questions are the Answers

Burke Hedges

- The Parable of the Pipeline

Dexter Yager

- Anything by Dexter
- Dexter's Business Builders
- Dynamic People Skills
- Ordinary Men Extraordinary Heroes
- Everything I Know at The Top I Learn At The Bottom

T. Harv Ecker

- Speed Wealth

Michael Clouse

- Recipe for Success (recording)
- Future Choice
- Learning the Business
- The Fifth Principle

Robert Kiyosaki

- The Business of the 21st Century (recording)
- The Business School

Tim Connor

- 52 Network Marketing Tips for Success, Wealth, & Happiness

Chris Weidner

- Any Chris Weidner

SCAN QR CODE FOR LINK TO THESE BOOKS ONLINE.

ELENA RAHRIG
INTERVIEWS
CAMI BAKER

10x Author
9x Academy Developer
4x Program Developer
International Consultant / Speaker
TransformMastermind.com

CONVERSATION WITH
OTTER PUBLISHING NEW YORK
(now Transform Publishing)

TransformMastermind.com/Publish

INTERVIEW WITH
RON SUKENICK

Ron Sukenick
RonSukenick.com
Public Speaker, Trainer, and Coach
Best Selling Author - Relationship Strategies &
LinkedIn Evangelist
National Expansion team for the
Gold Star Referral Clubs

INTERVIEW WITH
DIANE REYNOLDS